SECRETS

UNDER THE VEIL

EXPATS TELL ALL

Rose Gold Publishing, LLC

Other books written by Dr. Ana Gil Garcia include:

"*Textos Narrativos y Expositivos: Estrategias para la comprensión de la lectura en el currículo escolar*". 2nd edition. Co-author: Rosario Canizales. July 2010. ISBN: 0-9747416-0-4

"*El lector estratégico: De la teoría a la práctica*, [*The strategic reader: From theory to practice*]" Authors: Ana Gil, Ernestine Riggs, Rosario Canizales. Textbook. 2003. FEDUPEL, Caracas, Venezuela.

"*Helping Middle and High School Readers: Teaching and Learning Strategies across the Curriculum*" Authors: Ernestine Riggs and Ana Gil-Garcia, "*What We Know About*" Textbook series. Arlington, Virginia: Educational Research Services.

"*Textos Informativos y Expositivos: Estrategias para la Comprensión de la Lectura en el Currículo Escolar*" [*Expository and narrative texts: Reading comprehension strategies across curriculum*], Authors: Ana Gil García y Rosario Cañizales. Textbook. Chicago, IL: Robin Fogarty & Associates, 2003.

"*The principal as instructional leader: Teaching high school teachers how to teach reading*," Co-author: Dr. Ernestine Riggs, Bulletin: The Journal for Middle Level and High School Leaders, National Association of Secondary School Principals, October 1998.

Additionally, she has published twenty additional articles in refereed journals and ten in non-refereed journals.

She also Co-Authored the following with Mercedes Cardella, M. Ed.

"*Motivational Factors Leading Young Saudi Females to Become Bilinguals*", International Research in Higher Education, co-author: Mercedes Cardella, June 2017, online publication:
http://www.sciedupress.com/journal/index.php/irhe/issue/view/560

SECRETS

UNDER THE VEIL

EXPATS TELL ALL

Dr. Ana Gil Garcia &

Mercedes Cardella, M. Ed.

Rose Gold Publishing, LLC

Table of Contents

Prologue

"The Secrets Under the Veil: Expats tell all" book, a compilation of factual stories, reflects my journey for thirty years in the Kingdom of Saudi Arabia. As a Venezuelan plastic surgeon, my career took me across the U.S. and Europe often. Though my experiences were broad and varied, working in Saudi Arabia was never on the horizon, until I met my husband - "never say never." He had been working in Riyadh for ten years when we met and tried to explain the cultural shock and many social differences I would face. Young and in love, I was excited to come to Riyadh. The move was a significant adjustment; in all my travel, I never imagined I would be in another world entirely that felt like a separate bubble. Thirty years ago, I became the first female surgeon to practice in our Clinic in Riyadh. It seems that I will remain the only female foreigner physician until I retire from the clinic.

Each story in the book seems to mirror what my life has been in a country that I can call home. The personal narratives of the authors and their professional, social, cultural experiences are not far from what the reality of the day-to-day life environment women in Saudi still face. The book is arranged into five themes that explore culture shock, educational environment, social life, empowerment, and spirituality. With my extended living in the Kingdom, I could attest that the stories tell the expatriates' involvement, understandings, and encounters they have confronted. Those events may have challenged their social ways as they were continuously contrasting them with their western orientation.

By telling some of my personal stories, I expect that they can enforce and validate the stories based on facts that both women authors faced while they lived here. My experience working in Riyadh was full of hurdles. Unable to speak Arabic at the time, I had a translator for

the first years of my move. However, I was never certain the translation was accurate for my patient. Scheduled surgeries were often delayed because the women needed signed consent from their *Mahram*
(father, brother, husband, or son). I had never observed this delayed in any other surgical practice; the operation schedule is often tight and strictly adhered to this matter. However, Saudi women were not offended by this. They felt protected and right to be under the care of a man.

In the Arab culture, the roles of men and women are far more defined, and interaction between sexes is forbidden or frowned upon in certain areas. The marriage culture is very traditional, in that the majority of men look to marry a housewife to care for their home and take care of several children. When I first moved to the Kingdom, men occupied the vast majority of the job market, and women were unemployed. This made professional interactions in the workplace a novel and unique experience I would practice and develop daily. When I was introduced as a female physician to a man (physician or patient), I learned to wait and see if he extended his hand. If not, I would never shake hands; avoid physical and prolonged eye contact with him. These previous social codes were some of the most significant adjustments I needed to make as a trained Latin woman. As physicians, we would check on patients and families, often embracing any person we meet even. In Riyadh, our relationships were drier with our patients; I had to be accompanied by a nurse to enter an examination room and could not check on my patient by myself. I was advised to avoid discussions about religions and politics of the Middle East.

The Kingdom is recognized by both foreign prejudices and national resentment criticizing traditional laws and women's oppression. To my surprise, over the past decades, I have also come to see how Saudi women are accustomed to these societal and cultural norms, and many fear changes. This can be attributed to their faith, historical religious traditions, and the *Quran* (Islamic Holy Text) that serves as the government's constitution. However, in recent years, the Crown Prince Mohamad Bin Salman initiated reform projects. Some of those changes included allowing women to drive, granting tourist visas, allowing a single tourist woman to share her hotel room with her male partner, and for the hotel to not request proof of marriage. Also, to enable women to have the right to refuse the strict dress code (abaya, hijab, niqab).

Though there are several Islamic dominant countries in the region, the Saudi culture is one of a kind. Religion plays a critical part in their daily routine and thus regulates their cultural norms. Shops and businesses close five times a day for prayer, during which their call for prayer echoes from every mosque and can be heard everywhere in the city. At first, it was difficult to comprehend how a country can shut down multiple times a day. With time, I learned to build my schedule around their prayer regime. This is unique to Saudi culture. The majority of locals pause to convene and share in prayer. Not only is it a dry country, but it is also illegal for men and women to interact in public if they are not blood relatives. Consequently, socializing in public is rare, and gatherings are hosted in private homes.

My most exciting experience has been working with my Saudi colleagues, patients, males, and females from all different socioeconomic classes. My experience has been multi-dimensional. Due to the lack of female physicians and available practices in the region, I interact with a full spectrum of colleagues and patients every day - this trained patience, understanding, and an ability to comprehend I may not be able to communicate all the time fully. As a working professional in the Kingdom, your skills and character are continuously tested.

The "Secrets under the Veil: Expats tell all" book is an expression of a cultural reality that has started to change progressively. The challenges coped by the authors at the moment of their educational contracts in the higher education system here in Saudi summarize the inequities and unequal treatment females, not only expatriates but also nationals, have confronted for years. These imbalances are on the way for improvements, *inshallah*. The lessons learned after each story constitute an excellent glossary of wisdom and insights. The authors prudently avoid presenting their views and or judgments about each situation they experienced. Nevertheless, the stories captured accounts of conditions that can be compared to events I have personally experienced. They are legitimate narratives.

Overall, my experience working in Saudi Arabia and with Saudis has to be an added value to me personally and professionally. I applaud the new developments happening in the Kingdom, where women are more empowered, more socially connected, and overall more educated to lead.

Reading and writing the prologue about the "Secrets under the Veil: Expats tell all" transported me to my incredible journey in this country that I call home. My family, loved ones, friends, colleagues, and my medical practice have transformed the leadership I embraced and have expanded my cultural competencies. This has shaped who I am as a woman, a wife, a mother, a daughter, a friend, a colleague, and a spiritual practitioner.

Alida Harb Raide, M.D.
Board Certified Plastic Surgeon
Riyadh, Saudi Arabia

About the Author, Dr. Ana Gil Garcia

My life started in Margarita Island, Venezuela, many years ago. I am the oldest of seven siblings, and I completed my K-21 in Venezuela.

After working in the school system as a Science teacher, School District Supervisor, and Interim Superintendent of 210 schools, I left for the United States to complete my Master, Specialist, and Doctor of Education degrees.

My professional life has been full of unique and rich experiences, as I have received five different Fulbright Scholar awards.

As a scholar, researcher, community activist, human rights advocate, published author, and full professor at Northeastern Illinois University, I have traveled the world. I have taught as a visiting professor, training Junior Faculty, preparing teachers and school leaders, speaking at conferences, conducting research, doing humanitarian work, creating coalitions for Latino leadership parity, establishing digital bridges for minorities, but overall learning from others.

I have dedicated time to develop my infatuation for education and the multiple recognitions and awards - local, national, and internationally, has reaffirmed the work I do passionately.

I have been publicly recognized as one of the 100 Most Influential Hispanics in the USA, 50 More Influential Latinos in Chicagoland, 30 Outstanding Visionary Women in Higher Education to Distinguished Woman in Education, along with many other distinctions supporting my educational career.

I continue creating educational spaces for women and minorities to increase their academic opportunities.

A few of my proud accomplishments include serving in Humanity in Action, a worldwide Rotary International campaign to eradicate poverty, co-founding both ILCEL, a coalition to protect equity for Latinos in education, an IVA, an alliance to demand humanitarian awareness of Venezuelans facing human rights violations.

I profoundly believe that the next crusade of the century is to elevate the teaching profession across borders and to work collectively at all levels of education to make the world a better place.

About the Author, Mercedes Cardella, M. Ed.

I was raised in Toronto's east side borough.

As a child, I was exposed to a variety of cultures in my classroom, as many new immigrants called Scarborough their home.

Raised by a strong, single mother, she taught me what it meant to do more with the few available resources. She motivated and encouraged me to pursue my artistic talents and aim for the stars.

During my adolescent years, I attended Wexford Collegiate School for the Performing Arts, and I specialized in Musical Theatre. I continued to explore the performing arts throughout my undergraduate program at York University, where I majored in Political Science and History. During these years, I discovered my love for education and decided that upon completion of my undergraduate degree, I would teach English abroad.

Education provided me with a pathway to discover the world and make an impactful difference.

Teaching English as a second language has allowed me to live in several countries across Europe and the Middle East. As a professional educator, scholar, researcher, and published author, I have traveled and presented academic research papers at various universities worldwide.

Upon my return from the Kingdom of Saudi Arabia, I pursued my Master of Education at the University of Toronto. I was awarded the Ontario Graduate Scholarship (OGS) and graduated from the program with high distinction. Following my Master's degree, I am pursuing an ongoing career in film/television acting. I have produced several short films and have played principal roles in shorts and upcoming feature films.

My future goals include advancing in my acting career on an international level, advocating for the implementation of social justice and arts-based education within the curriculum, and starting a production company.

About the Illustrator, Enio Garcia Marin

Enio Garcia Marin, a Venezuelan artist, retired educator, and musician, has an extensive career as a plastic artist and cartoonist who has exhibited his work in different local and national museums. A well-known and celebrated cartoonist in local newspapers, his work is highly recognized as a historical and geographical muralist.

Many authors and singers in South America have used his designs for the covers of their books and music CDs.

His most recent painting work, "Retrospectiva de una Ciudad" [Retrospective of a City] are part of the leading exhibition of the Museum Francisco Narvaez in Margarita Island, Venezuela.

His long-life contributions to his homeland made him the recipient of the award, "Living Cultural Heritage" in 2013.

Introduction

We all travel for different reasons to places that most people already frequent. Nevertheless, not too many people go to geographical regions that are unknown to the rest of the world.

If someone were to choose a country to live in and start a life, Saudi Arabia would not be the first to come to mind.

In 2014, we left the North American continent, the United States and Canada, filled with anxiety for the unknown, and excitement for what we could accomplish at a new teaching position at a University, located in the Eastern Province of Saudi Arabia.

We spent two years of our lives in the Kingdom, and they were full of adventures and many misadventures. Nonetheless, those years spent in the desert were years of growth and overcoming self-imposed barriers. It was indeed an adventure of a lifetime, and we are grateful for the experiences and lessons that it taught us.

The announced arrival of potential educational reforms and the new adoption of state-of-the-art technology in the instructional classrooms in Saudi Arabia prompted us to respond to a worldwide advertisement requesting English-speaking educators from all over the world to apply for academic positions in Saudi's higher education institutions. The job description seemed the perfect fit for our educational desires of transforming youth lives through education and the willingness to endure the challenging environmental climate in the country. Yes, we both fit the mold!

In accepting the teaching positions in the Kingdom, we made assumptions that later proved to be difficult and troublesome.

The job descriptions we accepted offered substantial perks that were attractive to any educator with a certain degree of audacity and appetite for risk. It is essential to add that the 'once in a lifetime' opportunity has enticed foreigners to leave their native lands in exchange for lucrative salary incentives, free accommodations, health benefits, and an adventure of a lifetime. Sounds too good to be true, right? Well, each year, thousands of professionals from across the globe, resign their stifling jobs, and sign a minimum two-year contract to start their new lives in the Middle East. Yes, we said the Middle East.

We must also note that we had personal reasons to have agreed to the new academic journey ahead of us.
First, we both coincided with the mystery and fascination with a country that invites preconceived erroneous beliefs. For example, female independence, empowerment, and Saudi Arabia are three things that do not seem to go together; therefore, we wanted to know more about that intimate relationship from the perspective of an expatriate woman.

Second, our level of curiosity to learn what was behind the closed doors of the private nation of Saudi Arabia became an ignition point to decide to leave the comfort level of Chicago and Toronto. We left our homes, families, friends, and our work environment to embark on an adventurous journey.

We were also intrigued by the dress code that we were required to follow as women—the *abaya*—when out in public places. How would we look? How does it feel? What type of restrictions would the *abaya* enforce on us? What does it mean to conform to the Kingdom's rules of wearing a non-western dress for an extended period? The *abaya* is a necessary code that Saudi and Non-Saudi females must abide by regardless of the widespread belief that it might be optional.

We realized that we differ from our level of experience in education, a seasoned, and novice educator. One is on her way out of an enriched educational life, and the other one has entered the pleasant and rewarding career as an educator. The academic motivation driving us to temporarily leave our homes in Chicago and Toronto, to teach in a Saudi institution of higher learning for two years, were intentionally distinct.

The seasoned educator reflected upon the potential differences in educational practices implemented in the Saudi classrooms. On the other hand, the novice educator looked for something more fulfilling and exciting. She wanted to use her teaching credentials and obtain a position that would rekindle her passion for education, language, and the arts.

What we had in common was our limited facts, familiarity, understanding, and awareness of an educational system that had undergone reform and was actively recruiting native-English speaking professionals and subject matter experts to work in their universities and language institutes!

This book is a chronicle of our experiences living as expats in the Kingdom of Saudi Arabia. It contains a series of short stories that we wrote during our time there as a means of emotional catharsis and self-awareness.

The chapters are categorized into five major themes: Cultural Shock, Educational Environment, Social Life, Empowerment, and Spirituality.
Each tale, included in each section, concludes with a reflective component highlighting the lesson learned in each experience. After all, isn't that what life is all about - taking risks, making mistakes, and learning from it?

The final chapter reveals tips and recommendations that we have acquired for those interested in working and living in the Kingdom.

While compiling our stories, we had you in mind.

We thought of the open-minded reader that is curious to learn what it is like to live and work in Saudi Arabia. The professional woman, who picked up this book up by chance, and is looking to relocate to the Kingdom and advance her career; and to the women out there who struggle to open themselves up to vulnerability and taking chances, we hope that you can find a piece of yourself in these stories.

We want to clarify that this book is based on our personal experiences as expats living in Saudi Arabia and not from the standpoint of cultural, social, political, or religious authority. Also, to protect and respect the identities of individuals, places of business/institutions mentioned, aliases have been assigned.

On a final note, we offer our sincere gratitude to the many colleagues that have serendipitously come our way, in all shapes and forms. If it were not for those magical encounters, we would not have been able to find our authentic voices.

Ana & Mercedes

Culture Shock

There are many definitions of culture shock.

We are afraid to say that all of them are correct and aligned to the meaning of what a culture shock represents to anyone exposed to an unfamiliar culture, ways of life, local customs, different language, acceptable behaviors, and social attitudes.

In this book of stories, while living in the Kingdom, we adopted the following definition that entailed the theme of each story. The culture shock we refer to deals with feelings of uncertainty, confusion, or anxiety that we all experience with a new culture much different from your own.

We found that it also moved us from the typical process of being in love with what we were seeing and feeling when we first arrived in the Kingdom, to a level of frustration that things that we classified as standard were not occurring as we expected them to.

Also, we went through a stage of adjustment, which demanded us to internalize that we were living in another place that would be our new and substitute land for one or two years. Once we accepted this place, we began our plan to learn more about the new guidelines of the operation of the location we selected to temporarily call home.

We learned to cope with the new culture, and our mind and body started responding accordingly to the new living environment.

In this section, culture shock, you will also find stories related to food as a mechanism for relationships. Food is an expression of love in Saudi culture, and how the first dinner served with Arab food became a lifetime experience.

The family traditions also represented a culture shock. We tried to understand some social issues, such as the adoption of a child, attending a family affair such as a wedding. In addition, the rules of driving in a country in which women did not drive until recent events transformed the social tradition of having a driver. The culture shock also includes the visit of a family member and the shocking process to bring her to the Kingdom's land.

We explored interpersonal relations that produced culture shock as we analyzed the multiple facets of network ramifications we had with other expatriates, colleagues, higher administrators, local people, servants, drivers, and students, among different types of social relations.

We defined who an expatriate is; the closeness developed among expatriates and the development of incredible friendships with people of all lifestyles.

In this section, we shared stories on women's issues and the importance of beauty. The physical and cultural landscapes bring the reader to read stories on racial discrimination, including the shocking in-appropriateness of walking on your own in a shopping mall.

The theme culture shock closes with short stories of those unavoidable moments that were difficult to classify but were so important to mention since they constituted particular life experiences.

Being deprived of a glass of wine, learning about the death of a loved one while you are away, and passing as an Arab in an Arab nation are examples of stories that made us practice keeping an open mind with the new culture we selected to relocate temporarily.

Arrival to the Kingdom of Saudi Arabia

When I landed at King Fahd International Airport, I was beyond excited to get out of the plane after a grueling fourteen-hour flight. I got up from my seat and put on my *abaya* that I had purchased back in Toronto at an Islamic bookstore. It was not the most glamorous of *abayas*, but it sufficed. I gathered all of my belongings and exited the aircraft.

As I walked through the tunnel, my stomach felt like I had butterflies, and for the first time in a long time, I was nervous.

I followed the signs towards baggage claims and was mesmerized by all of the marble and granite that made up the airport. Everything was grand, and I can still remember the sweet smell of the warm climate mixed with scents of sandalwood and rose. Like a bloodhound, I kept sniffing the majestic scent that flowed throughout the airport, and I remember thinking, "This is what the Prophet ﷺ must have smelled like." I smiled and continued to follow the signs towards baggage claims.

Before I could gather my belongings, I had to go through customs, and there were at least thirty kiosks with only five custom officers in attendance. They were all wearing white *thobes* (a traditional garment worn by men in the Arabian Peninsula) and their red and white checkered *shemagh* (a traditional Arab headdress) and had their beards neatly groomed. They were all so handsome and yet intimidating.

I approached the officer with my passport on hand, and he looked at me and at the passport a few times. He had a stern look and did not say much. He finally broke his silence and said, "Look at the camera." I looked into the camera, like a deer in headlights, and my picture was taken. I wanted to ask if we could take another picture, but I didn't want to press my luck. He stamped my passport and handed it back to me and said, "Welcome."

"Thank you," I replied, grabbed my things from the counter, and walked away.

I continued my journey to collect my bags, and once I had all of my belongings, I proceeded towards the arrivals area.

Before my departure, my employer told me to look for a sign with my name on it as they would be sending out representatives from the university to retrieve me. I searched through the sea of faces of people picking up their families and friends, and I finally saw a sign held by a Saudi man with my name on it. I walked towards him and said, "I'm here."

He smiled and said, "Excellent, let me help you with your bags, and let's get going." He escorted me to a black SUV, Cadillac. I felt like the President, being accompanied to an important event. I climbed into the back seat of the car: it was air-conditioned and smelled like the scents I had just lusted over in the airport.

"Excuse me," I asked. "What is that smell, it smells good in here."

He replied, "It's *Oud*, here in Saudi Arabia: we always use *oud* or *bukhoor.*" I smiled and realized that my first item of business was to buy some *Oud* and spray it throughout my house.

After what felt like an eternity, we arrived at a big gate with guards armed with AK47s patrolling it. The driver showed his ID, and they let him through the first gate.

We continued driving and approached a secondary gate. I was starting to get nervous in the backseat and thought, what if I was being sold into prostitution? The guards came to my driver's window and asked him for his ID once again. He showed them his ID card and asked the driver to lower the backseat window so that they could see who was in the car. They glanced at me for a few seconds and then said, "Ok." The second gates opened, and palm trees and beautiful villas appeared.

The driver pulled up to the first villa and stopped the car. He popped open the trunk and took out my belongings. "Sister, welcome home," he exclaimed.

"This is for me?" I asked.

"Yes, this is your home." He gave me the key and instructed that I opened the door to my new home. I opened the door and searched for the lights. I turned them on, and a beautiful villa was revealed to me. All of the furniture was brand new and had the plastic cover over it. Completely in awe of my new accommodation, my driver brought me back to reality and said, "Tomorrow, you will take the 9 AM shuttle bus that will take you to the university for your orientation, ok?"

"Ok, thank you," I replied.

I closed my front door and looked at all of the space I had in my new home. I went into the master bedroom, and a king-sized bed with fresh new sheets and a gold-colored comforter awaited me. I dropped my purse on the floor and plopped myself onto it to test it out. It was so comfortable and inviting.

This was my new home, and I was excited to create some beautiful memories here.

Lesson: Real courage is to believe in yourself. Step out of your fears and follow your dreams.

My First Saudi Dinner

I had been in Saudi Arabia for only a week, and a few of my colleagues at work decided that it was time for me to experience a traditional Saudi feast. I had no idea what Saudi cuisine entailed, but I had heard that their portions were generous, and you wouldn't leave any Saudi house feeling hungry or unsatisfied.

A friend of mine made reservations for a few of us ladies to feast our hearts and mouths out at a renowned Saudi heritage restaurant. The restaurant immediately transported me back into traditional Bedouin Arabia. It was rustic, and there were monuments beautifully curated throughout the space. Arabian designed carpets spread across the floor in hues of burgundy and gold. A man wearing traditional Bedouin attire greeted us with fresh *Medjool* dates and gold embellished cups halfway filled with Arabic coffee.

I was curious as to why the cups were only filled halfway, and being the curious person that I am, I asked if my cup could be filled to the rim. The man smiled, and with his kind disposition, he replied, "It is Bedouin custom only to fill the cup halfway." He continued to say, "It means that we are welcoming you and want you to stay for as long as you'd like." Interesting, I thought, as I took a sip of the Arabic coffee. He explained that if a Bedouin pours you a full cup, they do not want you to linger around. We all laughed and continued sipping our Arabic coffee. "It's not like regular coffee; it has a bitter taste to it," I exclaimed. "This is why you have it with the bread of the desert," the man explained. "The dates sweeten the taste of the coffee, and your pallet begins to explore all of its dazzling possibilities." The amount of passion that this man had about his country, his culture, and the flavors of his native land was remarkable and left me famished for the main course.

The man escorted us to our private dining area, where there were traditional Arab couches aligned around the perimeter of the wall. The lights were dimmed to create a dramatic Arabian ambiance. There was an assortment of fresh juices and warm bread to munch on while we waited for our food to be prepared. My favorite was the lemon-mint drink, a staple in the Middle East.

A waiter came in and asked everyone which do they prefer, chicken or lamb? We all agreed with the chicken option. After a while, the waiter re-entered our private dining area and carried a large tray that smelled like heaven. He placed the tray in the middle of the room and said, "Enjoy!"

I looked over to my friends and asked, "This is all for us?" They laughed and nodded, yes. The amount of food on that tray could have fed an entire village. It was massive! "What is this dish called," I asked. "*Kabsaa*," replied one of our colleagues. "It's Saudi Arabia's national dish," another replied. "Don't we get plates and cutlery?" I asked.

One of the ladies replied, "No, this is a communal dish, so use your hands and dig in!" The rest of the crew began digging in with their hands, tearing pieces of chicken, and scooping up the rice with their hands. "You guys are serious," I replied. I knew that if I didn't get a piece of the action, I'd leave here hungry and cruelly taunted, so I dived in.

It felt strange eating with my hands, feeling the grain of rice in between your fingers, but after a while, I got used to it. There was a sense of connection and humility, as we shared this delicious dish. The tastes of different spices and flavors of cardamom were exploding in my mouth. We were unable to finish the large meal, but we left with our bellies full and an experience of a lifetime.

Lesson: Try new things and get out of your comfort zone.

Cooking is an Expression of Love and Patience

Food in the Kingdom is a matter of hospitality, friendship, religious ceremony, family celebration, and even bribery for a grade! Every culture links people through their food traditions.

In the Arab world, food conceptualizes what home is. One of my students invited me to have dinner at her home. She said, "My grandmom is cooking." She asked me about my favorite Arab meal, and I admitted that I did not have any in particular. I found that although there were many commonalities in the Arab food among Middle Eastern countries, the opposite was also correct about each country having a specific dish that would make the country different from others.

I did make it clear that I was open to trying any type of food except those dishes containing red meat. She started listing vegetarian dishes and mentioned *Kusaa Mahshee*, a traditional Arab dish consisting of stuffed zucchinis. I learned that this dish does not have a specific recipe because it is made out of love and patience that the cook puts into making the food.

I was ready at 5:00 pm on a Saturday, and just when I was about to call my driver, I heard a knock at my door. When I opened it, an Indian man asked for my name. He said that he was the chauffeur of the family and that they have sent him to pick me up.

I was a bit surprised and confused since I did not arrange a ride with my hosts. I reacted with the proper fears of a Westerner, thinking about rape, kidnapping, etc.!! I called my hosts to verify.

I arrived at my dinner invitation expecting many members of the family. However, my student, her sister, and their grandmother were the only family members waiting for me. They wanted to know about me, my children, my personal and professional background, among other details of my individual life story.

While I was speaking, a maid came and brought yellow tea with mint in it, dates, sweets, and chocolates. The server was a Filipina contracted by the family for three years through a government program that brought them to work across the Kingdom as housekeepers.

One hour after my arrival, I was asked to go to the dinner table. The table was utterly replete of plates with different types of Arabic dishes, primarily fish, chicken, rice, yogurt, potatoes, seafood, and dates. Traditionally, Arabic cuisine relied mainly on local ingredients available along the Arabian Peninsula, such as wheat, dates, rice, barley, and meat, making their meals a healthy choice.

When I asked for particular dish ingredients, I understood that when Arabs cook for guests, they do more than preparing a meal; they put their love and appreciation into the art of cooking.

I also learned that food is perceived as a mechanism for breaking barriers with expatriates. At the table, they used both a fork and a knife, but they also used their hands.

My curiosity increased during dinner as I found out that food could interpret their frustrations and losses, demonstrating their trust and comfort, and triggering family memories.

Lesson: The cultural value of food is immense as you are open to others' meaning of the same dish.

Who are the Expatriates?

In the countries of the Middle East, no one is an immigrant. We are all expatriates, hereafter referred to as *expats*. Another word used to define who we are as a foreigner.

The people I met went to the Kingdom for different reasons. No one story was similar to another.

Interacting with faculty, administrators, staff, janitors, and drivers made me think that the only thing that we all had in common was financial concerns.

Some of us believed that salaries in Saudi were higher than in the United States. Other people from the States accepted job positions for saving purposes and avoided paying taxes if they stayed 335 consecutive days. Others had family reasons such as divorces, broken relationships, loss of a close family member, alcoholism, drug addiction, among others.

In my case, I went with a specific reason in my mind- to save money to pay for my daughters' destination wedding.
When we met, expatriates, especially females, we all talked about our loved ones back in our countries of origin.

I cannot begin to elaborate or establish a profile of a type of individual inclined to spend time away from home, in an environment 360 degrees different from theirs; with very little interaction with the exterior world, wearing clothes far different from theirs, and decide to adapt to cultural circumstances not favorable for women.

It is relevant to describe some of the characters that were now our new colleagues. We learned to cohabit with them, without previous knowledge of who they were before and what they did in their lives back home.

One of the administrators, a chairperson, was a cat lover. She has more than ten cats. The cats run the house. They sit and sleep on the couches and eat healthy food for cats. She was a very religious woman who likes to gather people at home to study the bible. Because of her extreme religious fanaticism, I heard she invited others for prayer at her house to avoid President Obama from being elected to a second term!

Also, many of us attended her Thanksgiving dinner, an Eastern celebration, a Christmas holiday, among other gatherings. Most people in the compound always expected parties at her house because of her openness, collegiality, generosity, and the friendliness she transpired. Most of her academic life had taken place in Saudi. For now, she expects to retire from a Saudi institution since her possibilities of being hired in the United States have decreased considerably.

Another faculty colleague left the United States after a bankruptcy. She accepted the position in the Saudi institution due to her financial situation.

She was not a social person. She was an introvert, a very reserved individual, who others intentionally researched and later learned about her personal and professional lives. Unfortunately, she believed that no one knew the reason for her relocation outside the States.

One of the administrators, who later and suddenly deflected from the institution to go to another Saudi one for higher pay, was a foreigner with a divorce story forced by the circumstances of falling in love with one of his students. His student was 21-years old, as old as his oldest daughter. This Nordic citizen was 54-years old. He ran away from his town of residency and his family due to social pressures from his academic environment.

Another faculty, a Caucasian female, a horse lover, was away from her husband and her family for almost three years. She did not go home periodically, but she used her time off for Spring and or Ramadan breaks to travel around the neighboring Middle Eastern countries.

All expats have unique stories of success or failure. Learning about the expats' stories became the frame of reference to our own story. Many stories can be told about multiple people with great character and diverse personalities who made the day to day life more interesting and more comfortable to carry on.

Lesson: The definition of family is transformed in other latitudes by the hierarchy of your personal needs and wants.

Expat Friendships

The expats are a tight-knit community, and generally speaking, everyone knows everyone.

Typically, your employer—who is also your sponsor—provides you with your accommodations. If you choose to live in the housing provided by your employer, you will live with a lot of your colleagues.

Accommodations were assigned as single, shared, or family. I had the privilege of being a single female, living in a villa. These villa accommodations were reserved for upper management personnel, but I was somewhat "lucky" to get a villa all to myself. I guess I had what Saudi's would call *wasta*—a term used to express that one is profoundly connected.

The Kingdom is all about networking, and it is essential to make the right friendships and the right connections.

During my time in the Kingdom, I made some fantastic friendships that will be forever cherished. Many of which I visit and talk to regularly. We spent an incredible amount of time together. We worked, shopped, traveled, ate, cried, and laughed with these beautiful people. They become the support that you need to get you through any adversity.

I realized that I shared more than just work and the compound with these individuals. In many instances, the bond that was formed between expats was sacred, and those friendships turned into family.

Being away from family during the holidays can be very challenging, and expats make up for that void. The expat experience allows you to celebrate Western holidays together so that you don't feel isolated.

As a Canadian, I was able to celebrate two Thanksgivings! It was one of the most rewarding experiences in living and teaching abroad. When you become an expat, you meet some fantastic people that come from all walks of life and have interesting stories of their own.

Lesson: You can create beautiful memories with the friends you meet in the Kingdom.

The Shuttle Network

Faculty, Filipino staff, and drivers become your day-to-day close network in Saudi. The university shuttle served as the networking environment to initiate any close interactions.

You quickly learned who took the shuttle earlier or later, who sat together and who reserved a seat for someone. You also verified stories or rumors about who suddenly disappeared from the university without informing the academic authorities of their intention to resign.

The shuttle also functioned as a debriefing on what happened in the classroom on a particular day. It was the venue for social engagements. People driving in the shuttle used their time to complete their grading or to make phone calls back home because of the time change.

Faculty differentiated from administrators because they drove on the bus, and the administrators were given university cars only if they were males.

We all knew when someone was taking a vacation, where that person was going, and who they were going with. Shopping plans were made while inside the bus. The latest sales in the mall and the discovery of a new restaurant formed part of the conversations as well.

On the bus, we knew how many cats someone was feeding. The stories of our families, children, and significant others became our stories. We shared happy and sad moments. Others could perceive the initial relationship between two expatriates as they always sat aside, one waited for the other one, or they got off at the same place.

Many family moments became everybody's celebration. For example, some of those moments included graduation ceremonies, children, weddings, family celebrations, broken relationships from back home, and many other life events.

We created favoritism with the shuttle drivers. Some of them were very personal but did not speak English. When necessary, we complained about the driving by some of our drivers, and three of them were terminated. Some were replaced because of their careless way of driving, speeding, and violating other traffic rules. The shuttle was the best platform for social networking!

Lesson: Don't take for granted the lasting communication effects of the villagers of your temporary community.

A Saudi Friendship

Saudi's are very private people and prefer to keep their circles intimate.

I worked with a Saudi female instructor, and it took her a little over a year to finally say hello to me. It was during our language exchange lunch program, and on that particular day, none of the students showed up, and we decided to use that hour as a way to introduce ourselves to one another. We instantly connected, and she told me a little about her life. She was a Saudi who had studied in the US for several years and returned to KSA with her family.

She lived a privileged life, as her father held a high-profile position for the largest oil company in the world, ARAMCO. After several weeks of chatting with each other at work, she invited me to her home. I remember being incredibly excited that I was going to see what a Saudi home looked like. I had my driver take me to her house, and she opened the door, hugged me, and welcomed me. She had prepared Arabic coffee, dates, an assortment of pastries, and snacks. Saudi's are unbelievably hospitable. It's ingrained in their culture to be so. We watched movies and shared stories, and our bond quickly grew into a beautiful friendship. She became such an important person in my life, and I am happy that we both decided to discover each other and become friends. My only regret is that we hadn't begun our friendship sooner.

Lesson: Make friends with the locals. It's a shame to leave Saudi Arabia without having gained a Saudi friend.

Mourning a Friend from Away

Today my word is sorrow. The different expressions of sadness, desolation, and sorrowful manifested by Saudis due to the death of King Abdullah makes me think he will be missed for a long time. But also, today, I learned about the passing of a great woman, educator, and friend: Dr. Ann Grey. After fighting cancer for a long time, she passed away.

Ann was a great educational consultant, and I had the privilege to share the academic stage with her many, many times. It was fun. She was fun! "I will keep you in my heart, Ann."

Unfortunately, today, I also learned about another friend that also passed away. He briefly came into my life.

We used to do the "pequeñas cosas" (small things) that Joan Manuel Serrat, the Spaniard singer, described in his poem/song. His outgoing personality also deserved a segment of the Alberto Cortes' poem/song *"Cuando un amigo se va"* (when a friend is gone) …Yes, he left an empty space, as the song said.
Since I was living by myself, no one was around to talk to immediately, any sad news I received while away, was maximized by the solitude of this place. It made me reflect on how minuscule and vulnerable we all are. The decision I made to leave my country and to live on my own is always on my mind when I go to bed. It was terrifying to think that anything could happen to me at any time. My fear increased as I heard stories of expatriates who found dead a few days after other colleagues realized that they had not seen them getting on the bus or being absent from teaching.

Two months ago, one of our American colleagues living in the male compound was reported missing. Three days later, a neighbor heard his cat crying and decided to knock at his door. It was earlier in the morning on a Saturday. The incessant crying of the cat made her go to the security office. When they came and opened the door, he was lying on the floor of his bathroom. Would it be possible that his life could have been saved? Who knows? When I think about that and other cases that people talk about, I realize that I need to make sure that at least two people know when I am home or if I am traveling.

Lesson: Living in another country temporarily teaches you that friendship is momentary, transitory and short-lived. Nostalgia

Escorted Out of the Mall

Every Sunday afternoon, faculty and staff living together in the same compound (gated neighborhood), were picked up by a university bus to do our two hours of grocery or other types of shopping.

We drove to the mall. After doing my grocery shopping, I decided to venture out and walked alone inside the mall. I was window shopping. I did not get too far before being stopped by the moral police patrolling the mall.

I was admiring the uniqueness of the beautiful designs of evening dresses when two police officers, dressed in their traditional man *dishdasha* or *thobe* and their head *shemagh*, asked for my *hijab* (veil) and why I was by myself in the mall. When I responded, both men realized I was not Arab and that I was an expatriate. Unfortunately, being an expatriate did not stop them from escorting me out of the mall without reservation.

I want to make it clear that regardless of your residency status, female foreigners must be accompanied by someone else when going out and must wear the abaya, not the hijab (veil). Showing our head, face, and hair constitute the only sign of identity that we, female expatriates, can preserve in a society being ruled by Islamic principles.

Lesson: Regardless of where you are, respect the land's social rules because they are important pieces of the cultural values of the country.

My Driver

———————➤ ● ◄———————

Adnan was my regular driver and pretty much my lifeline in KSA. He took me to run my errands, helped me with my groceries, and served as my local guide. He would take me to his favorite Pakistani restaurant, where he would order chicken *boti* to munch on during our adventures. Whenever I was feeling down and out, he'd get me *Kashmiri* or *Karak* chai from my favorite tea sommelier. He became a confidant and someone I could depend on to help me navigate through the Kingdom. It was unbelievable how much time I spent with my driver. He knew everything, including all the gossip hailing out of our workplace. He knew things that were happening at my work before I even knew and would always fill me in with the latest scoop.

Adnan always had a smile, larger than life, but I could tell he was hiding something. He was unhappy. His wife had passed away during the birth of their second child, and he lived with a tremendous amount of guilt. As I mentioned before, we spent a lot of time together, and our exchanges gradually grew, and he opened up to me. He told me that he was grateful for the opportunities that living in KSA had given him, but he wanted to get remarried and eventually return to Pakistan.

A little over a year of getting to know each other, he professed his love and admiration for me and asked me to be his wife. I respectfully declined and told him it just could not be possible. We lived different lives, and I didn't plan on relocating to Pakistan. Regardless of my decision, he continued to pitch marriage and Pakistan and told me that I wouldn't have to work and that I would live a good life there.

Unfortunately, I quickly grew impatient with him as he began to pressure me into marrying him, and I felt sad. Sad, because I knew this would be the end of our friendship. I kept thinking to myself, "Why does this keep happening to me?" Could it be the sexual tension that exists here? Does it propel people to make such irrational decisions? I knew that if I kept seeing Adnan, it would make for a truly uncomfortable situation. I switched drivers. It was for the best.

Lesson: Drivers are the gatekeepers of the Kingdom's secrets.

What is Wrong with Having a Driver?

While in Saudi, all females were not allowed to drive and were only permitted to be in a car adequately identified and certified to drive a woman alone. The new King recently changed that law. Women are now allowed to drive in Saudi Arabia.

We all had drivers, but they were not exclusive drivers for only one female. We shared our drivers. They established their schedule to drive us whenever we needed to go to places for shopping reasons, medical appointments, social gatherings, restaurant outings, trips to Bahrain, among other things.

A foreigner that ignores the cultural reality of the woman in KSA would assume that they are restrained and limited to drive. However, we do not think about the effect of traditions and family values and standards that characterize cultures. The Kingdom of Saudi Arabia is not an exception.

My students were all born in the Kingdom. They were between 17 to 20 years old. They have always lived in Saudi with their parents. All of them had a chauffeur. Many of them were born with one who transported them and their moms everywhere they went. It would be inconceivable to think about having a permanent driver all of your lifetime. However, it is only unimaginable if you had been born outside Saudi Arabia.

Driving is a natural skill in the western hemisphere. Women and men do not have restrictions to drive. By a certain age, women are expected to learn how to drive as a sign of independence. The most common societal practice around the world would probably be driving not to be affiliated with gender.

Driving is considered a skill for a routine task. We can rationalize the importance of driving for all. Still, we must accept that reasons infused in the culture weigh essential reasons to do or not to do things established by the cultural and social environment, including family.

I still remember the day when King Abdullah passed. The news of his death spread rapidly. The educational institutions made provisions immediately to comply with the national mourning of the beloved King. The King's cause of death was pneumonia. The King was 90 years old. He was the third wealthiest head of state in the world, with a personal fortune estimated at US$18 billion.

On the morning of January 24, 2015, the university community received the news that due to the King's passing, the institutions, public and private, were to remain closed as long as the funeral services lasted.

The same morning, TV stations around the globe announced that women were allowed to drive in Saudi Arabia as of that day. This announcement was false.

We all took the news with joy, not for us expats, but for the Arabic females who had presumably waited for a long time to be able to drive. With that new information in mind, I went to my classroom and showed my contentment. Joyfully, I commented on the news that Saudi women were finally allowed to drive. Shortly after, one of my students asked me what was wrong with having a driver? I was not expecting that question because I was ready for open support for the critical event. My reality hit me. My cultural competency fooled me again.

They were born and raised with a driver. They did not know any other way of transporting themselves from one side of town to another except with a personal driver. Yes, why would they need to drive when someone traditionally did that for them. The misconception that because driving worked for western females, a Saudi female must adapt to it, was wrong and misconstrued.

Lesson: Changes are easily embraced if there are tangible benefits.

Orphans for Adoption

Learning and knowledge come your way every day.

Today, as I listened to one of my Writing Research freshman students, I learned about some adoption practices in Saudi based on Islamic guidelines. I learned that less than 2% of orphans are adopted in Saudi Arabia. Yet contradictory to the Prophet's actions, the student said, the Quran provides different interpretations about adoption. For example, an adopted child will not be eligible to inherit from his adoptive parents. Only blood-related children have that right. Also, the adopted child will always be called by his/her biological father's last name.

Regarding gender, if a boy is adopted and nursed by his new mother, she will be considered *mahram* of the child, which means that she will not have to cover her head when the child grows. On the contrary, if a boy is adopted and is not nursed, the mother and female non-blood relatives will have to cover their heads before him forever.

When girls are adopted, they must cover their heads when interacting with any of the males in her adoptive family. Lastly, because the adopted child is not a blood relative, it is acceptable to consider marriage between him/her and a close member of the family. One consequence of these Islamic adoption practices is that Saudi nationals refrain from adopting a child to prevent future family complications. Therefore, Orphan children keep growing in the Saudi orphanages, unbelievable!

Lesson: All human beings deserve the same and equal set of rules of day-to-day life.

Cannot Talk About Domestic Abuse

The beauty of Saudi women's research conducted by my students brought beauty and understanding to my soul. The topics of their studies made me sometimes pause because I was not sure about the waters that I, as a classroom faculty, was navigating. I was afraid of the potential implications for my profession and my life. I could not stop the research eagerness of my students to learn more about social issues affecting their daily lives. Two of the topics of concern were domestic violence and rape.

Although unethical to reveal the specifics of the research studies conducted by my female students, I can elaborate in general terms to indicate that we all make wrong assumptions about the existing domestic violence in countries with very rigid and scrupulous societies like Saudi.

The heated discussions in the classroom on family violence raised awareness on the number of cases that go unrevealed due primarily to, religion and family tradition.

The young age for marriage between a woman and a man and the hierarchical type of relationship imposed seems to facilitate the increasing and systematic acts of domestic violence at home.

It is an issue of power between a man over a woman. The male population has the right to select their women regardless of age. The fact that one man can have several wives would favor domestic abuse at home. All women protect each other but cannot denounce the abuser at any time. Most women know different stories and know someone who is and had been abused, not only physically but sexually.

Two of the research papers revealed the male guardianship system existing in Saudi. It means that the life of a Saudi female is compromised from the moment she is born until her final days of life. The system imposes that every woman must have a male guardian, usually her father, her brother, her husband, and in some cases, her son. They have the power to make many critical decisions on a woman's behalf. This system is one of the major impediments for women's development and independence. It is also one of the significant reasons Saudi women are fleeing the country.

The guardianship system encourages domestic violence and makes it challenging to seek protection or to have access to social services. The presence of male relatives for any of these acts would be considered an encouragement by the government to abuse women domestically.

My students were conducting research studies on social themes facilitated to learn about the intimacy of forbidden issues, such as domestic violence, which is also known as family violence.

One phrase in one of the papers that stuck with me was: "domestic family abuse in the Kingdom is not a gender issue; it is a human issue."

Lesson: You can hide your injured face but not your wounded soul.

Experiencing a Wedding!

I went to a Saudi wedding celebration of one of my 20-year old students.

The opulence and luxury of the evening started at 9:30 pm. It is customary for men and women to celebrate the wedding separately.

Usually, the wedding party is where Arab moms pick up the future bride for their sons! At this fantastic wedding, I learned that there is no civil union in KSA and no minimum legal age for marriage.

Before the final celebration arrives 6 to 12-months after the proposal/engagement, several steps are taken. First, the prospective groom's senior family leader informs the prospective bride's mother of his intention, and both families determine the suitability of the marriage. If agreed, the *Shawfa* (the viewing of the uncovered bride by her future husband) is approved by both families. Immediately after, Milka (a contract) is signed. The Mahr (bride price) is much higher for a virgin than for a divorcee or widow.

The wedding celebration (*Zawaj*) is a fashion show and a contest of haute couture by Saudi women to display their exquisite and exotic evening gowns.

At the wedding, the women took the floor to dance with sensual movements. The expatriate female servants, dressed in gold and white, distributed the diverse variety of sweets, especially chocolates, juices, tea, and Arab coffee for two hours.

The bride arrived closer to midnight with her father. Before she entered, women were informed that the father and the groom, (two males), were coming to the female celebration so that they would cover their faces and bodies with their *abayas* until the males would leave the room.

The wedding party was composed of the closest family of the bride and the groom. They all marched together ceremoniously. The newlywed couple did walk behind the parents. It was interesting that the bride was the only female allowed to be uncovered in the room. The couple sat for a long time in a particular place, facing the female audience.

The wedding pictures were taken, the family lined up, and closest friends were allowed to come closer to congratulate the couple. Immediately after, the couple cut the cake, had more pictures, and left the room to go back to the male side. Huge screens located in the room showed the men dancing in the other room.

The bride joined the rest of the males. They were now allowed to see the unveiled face of the bride under the permission of both parents. The extravagant dinner was served on the female side, at midnight.

By then, and after eating an immense quantity of sweets and drinking a lot of tea, food was not attractive anymore!

Lesson: *Do not interpret others' world of fantasies when yours is contaminated with cultural opinions.*

My Mother's Visit to KSA

Leaving my mother and family behind for the very first time in my life was one of the hardest things I had to do.

Going half-way across the world to a country that has garnered a terrible international reputation was not something my mother was raving about. She had her concerns, and as a mother, you would be protective of your child. My mother is not the overbearing type and always encouraged me to find my path and my voice in this world.

If it were not for her strength and inspiration, I would not have had the courage to go to the Kingdom in the first place.

My mother always inspired me, and for that, I am eternally grateful for her. When I had settled in and collected my bearings, my mother suggested coming to visit me in the Kingdom. Her curiosity and her motherly instincts of wanting to see if her daughter was living the way she described it to her became the stimulus for her to make arrangements to come and visit me.

She applied for a family visa, and I sponsored her through the help of the human resources department at my institution. Several months of back and forth bureaucratic procedures and *"Inshallah's"* later, I was able to fly my mother on Emirates and greet her at the King Fahd International Airport in Dammam. We embraced each other and let out tears of joy, excitement, and exhaustion.

In true mama bear fashion, she kissed me and said: "I'm hungry, where are those Kebabs!" I laughed and told her a tasty assortment of Mixed grill, fresh hummus, *fattoush* (Lebanese salad), and warm bread was waiting for her at home to devour.

When we arrived at my house, she smiled and looked over to me and said, "This house reminds me of Sicily." We laughed and filled our bellies with love and good food. My mother spent a total of ten days in the Kingdom, and each day was filled with adventure.

She rode a camel for the very first time and nearly fell off of it! She visited the caves of Al-Hasa, where it is believed to be the caves written in the story of Ali Baba and the forty thieves.

She wore an elegant customized *abaya* and confessed that she could get used to wearing one. My mother dined in fancy restaurants. She experienced her first gold souk adventure, visited heritage museums, and walked freely in the malls. She conversed with locals and realized that the media was portraying them to be monsters. She was impressed with their humility and hospitality, even though a grandiose environment surrounds Saudi's. She wished she could have extended her stay. Those ten days passed quickly. My mother left Saudi Arabia with peace of mind and her heart full. It is a memory that I will cherish forever.

Lesson: Let your loved ones know that you're okay. If they don't believe you, show them.

Love for Cats

Islam holds a special place for cats. The domestic cat is a revered animal in Islam, admired for its cleanliness. It is believed that the Prophet Muhammad gave sermons with *Muezza*, his beloved cat. Mistreating a cat, therefore, is seen as a severe sin.

My story is about a cat found dead in my laundry room. Each house had a private laundry room in the backyard. My home was not an exception. One day, I went to my laundry room to wash my clothes.

As I opened the door, the odor coming from inside was unbearable. A cat was dead between the dryer and washing machines. It may have been dead for more than seven days, so it was decomposed and decayed. I inferred that the cat got trapped inside and did not know how to get out and died from starvation.

It was a Friday, who can I call for help? No one is around on Fridays because it is prayer day. The silence in the compound was sepulchral. I knocked on several doors, but nobody responded. Finally, I rang the doorbell of a Swedish neighbor. He opened his door, I told him about the dead cat, and he looked at me and sincerely said: "The Prophet Muhammad said that your punishment on the Day of Judgment would be torture and hell," and closed his door!

Those were my neighbors: very different from the Mexican's "Vecindad del Chavo" - no sense of community!

I went home thinking about what I had done to deserve to be punished by the Prophet. With my Western mindset, I was more concerned with hygiene, cleanliness, and festering of bacteria that cause illnesses as opposed to the symbolic meaning of the cat in Islam.

I waited after prayer time was over, and I asked one of the Pakistani workers in the compound to come and help me clean the laundry room. For three dollars, he picked up the cat, washed the room thoroughly, and mopped with lavender detergent to kill the bad odor. Later, as I was still under the impression that I had sinned, I navigated the internet to learn more about the meaning of the cat in Islam. I learned that the cat is a revered animal admired for its cleanliness as well as for being loved by the Islamic Prophet Muhammed. A cat is considered "the quintessential pet" by Muslims, according to Wikipedia.

Lesson: Do not play with traditional beliefs and popular misconceptions if you want to survive in a cultural environment plague with morality restrictions.

The Art of Persuasion

As a woman in a patriarchal society, I realized that a Western feminist mentality would not get you what you desire in the Kingdom. Contrary to popular belief, Saudi women are not oppressed and submissive beings. For the most part, they are cunning and have mastered the art of persuasion. They have tastefully mastered the skill of persuasion and can get men to do practically anything for them.

I met a highly intelligent and beautiful Saudi woman by the name of Ghazal. We worked together, and I would often vent in her office about the bureaucratic injustices that I was experiencing. I recall telling her that it was hard to work with a system that was foreign to me. Things didn't work like the way they did in Canada. Ghazal told me to think differently. "Surely, things will not happen for you if you continue to think the way you think," she exclaimed. "You can get anything you want; you just have to learn how to listen."

At the time, I couldn't help but think that her "fortune cookie proverbs" would serve to be useless. I decided to test her approach that afternoon with the department of housing. When I arrived home, I visited the housing management office and requested to have an issue resolved. Naturally, I would have crossed my arms and glared at the manager with a stern look to make my point. I decided to approach this gentleman with kindness, a sense of grace, and calmness. I told him how appreciative I was for his assistance. My issue was resolved by the end of that evening.

Lesson: You can get whatever you want in life. You have to learn how to read people and learn the art of listening and persuasion.

Forgot to Wear Mascara!

I was scheduled to teach a class at 8:00 am. More than 35 minutes after I started my class, and students were engaged in an activity, a student arrived and went to sit directly without apologizing for her lateness. When the session ended, she came to see me and said that she wanted to tell me a "female secret" that had happened to her before coming to class. Of course, as a woman, I thought that she had a "monthly accident," her menstruation that unexpectedly stopped her from being on time. She looked at me and said that she asked her driver to go back because she had forgotten to put her mascara on. I thought that I heard "mascara," and I interpreted the word as a Spanish word for "mask." I said, "wow, you use the same word that we use in Spanish for a mascara" Naively, I asked her, "Do you have a Halloween party?"

She said, "No, Dr. Ana. I forgot to put mascara on my eyebrow, and today, Thursday, we communicate via cell phone with the boys in the male building. They see our faces. I cannot show my eyes without mascara."
So, she was late to class because it was more important to show her beautiful face to the prohibited fruit, the boys, without mascara. I thought about priorities in life; I smiled. I also thought about the importance of co-ed education, in which males and females see each other every day in a more relaxing atmosphere because they are not in a wedding contest.

Saudi Arabia is the largest market for cosmetic products in the Middle East and Africa. The country has one of the world's highest consumption rates of cosmetics and is the leading country in the consumption of skin and hair care.

In Saudi, two cities have the largest younger population - Jeddah and Riyadh. In both cities, young girls spend a lot of money on their appearance. No surprise that my student was one of the many who valued her mascara more than coming to class on-time! But I could not dismiss the purpose behind wearing mascara: a virtual date through a technology mechanism that is rapidly facilitating the interaction between males and females in a forbidden environment.

Lesson: As more restrictions are imposed on others, the more creative they become to violate them.

The Lost Woman

Have you ever stared in the eyes of a lost woman? A woman whose soul has been ripped apart into pieces.

During my first few weeks in the Kingdom, I met a woman named Diana. She was the kind of woman that lived in the past. She romanticized about her previous experiences in the Kingdom a few years earlier and decided to leave the US for good in search of love and happiness.

As I got to know her over a cup of Arabic coffee and dates at a local café, she informed me that she had met a Pakistani man in America, and he used her for American citizenship status. His intentions were to bring his true love to America and begin a family with her. Saddened by her experience, Diana decided to leave behind her life in America and make her way to what she called it, "the land of princesses."

As I sat there looking at her, I could see the pain mixed with a sense of delusion in her eyes. "I want to find myself a rich Saudi, and be treated like a princess," she exclaimed. Was this a thing? Were American women fleeing America in search of their Arabian prince charming? Were they envious of the lifestyles that some of these Saudi women lead? I was curious to know more about this phenomenon. She took a sip of her coffee and looked at me with a piercing look. "You will marry a rich Saudi. You're young, beautiful, and desirable." Her eyes filled with envy. I realized Diana was a woman filled with regrets and needed an opportunity to make up for her past.

Lesson: The two thieves of life: regret for the past and fear of the future.

A Filipino Name

"Your name looked Filipino," that was the argument given to exclude me from a list of US citizens who live in the Eastern Province of Saudi Arabia. The list is created to inform US citizens about cultural, social, and even potential threat events that happen in the region.
Even in foreign lands, the discrimination follows us, Latinos!

The US Embassy is considered the only place where US citizens would enjoy a concert, drink a glass of wine, and or wear a Halloween costume. None of these social events are allowed in the Kingdom.

For that reason, US citizens expect to be on the list of the Embassy to enjoy the forbidden activities that are not part of the social interaction that an expat would have elsewhere. White Americans control the list of the Embassy.

One of my colleagues from South Africa told me about the list, the parties, the entertainment, seminars, among other activities that the US Embassy plans annually. She gave me the name of the person I needed to speak to. I went to see her and requested information on how to be added to the list. She looked at me intensely and asked, "Are you an American?"

I said, "Yes, I am."

With disdain, she said, "I am sending your name to the US Embassy, but I wouldn't be surprised if your Latino name is confused as a Filipino one." As expected, I was not invited to any social event. My name looked Filipino!

The influx of Philippine nationals is very high in Al Khobar. They are workers doing different jobs, either technical, construction, or housekeeping work. India, Pakistan, Philippines, Malaysia, and Indonesia constitute the labor force primarily in Saudi Arabia.

The history of the Philippines has traces in Spain. For centuries, the Spanish conquered and colonized the country and forced the Philippines to adopt as surnames, what we consider Ibero American last names: Garcia, Gonzales, Rodriguez, etc. Of course, their first names are also our names: Ana, Maria, Monica, Mercedes, Marta, Veronica, etc. The discrimination in Khobar against the Philippines is severe. They are considered third-class citizens. Their salary is meager, their contractual conditions are stringent and inhumane, and their socialization is minimal by the places that they are allowed to go. However, they have created their mafias, circles, and groups. They know what to buy and where to go to get lower prices. They are extremely friendly and always willing to help. They are transient human beings forced to leave their country due to the critical poverty they face. Every Friday afternoon, long lines of Filipinos stand at the Western Union to send their salaries to their home country to support those who they left behind.

Lesson: Racial discrimination is transported by others based on their own prejudices.

Female Travel in the Kingdom

Contrary to popular belief, females can travel freely throughout the Kingdom without the accompaniment of male guardianship. However, I must specify that expat women have more freedom to travel freely, as opposed to Saudi women. Some conservative Saudi families may refrain from having their daughters or wives travel freely, while less traditional families are open to it.

Apart from Saudi Arabia being the birthplace of Islam, the Kingdom houses some of the most beautiful historical and archeological sites of the world. The edge of the world, *mada'in saleh* (the Petra of Saudi Arabia), the empty quarter and Farasan Islands are just a few examples of the beautiful gems in Arabia.

I lived in the Eastern province, so I was close to the neighboring country Bahrain, a destination where expats and locals would indulge in their vices for the weekend.

I was able to travel and see a lot of the country with my friends, which included males who had access to transportation. We drove throughout the entire country on weekends and would stay with fellow expat friends in other cities.

You can take a train from Damman to Riyadh, which takes about four hours and explore the capital city. The train is safe, clean, and inexpensive. When I traveled alone, I did not experience any harassment in the Kingdom. Generally speaking, Saudi men are respectful and usually keep to themselves. They are not as forward as other men may be from neighboring Arab nations.

Unfortunately, harassment is a worldwide phenomenon, and as a female solo traveler, prepare yourself for the unexpected "catcalls" in any country that you are traveling to. As I write this, I realize that Saudi Arabia is going through a tremendous amount of societal changes, and tourist visas are speculated to be granted to various countries around the world. It is a beautiful nation, rich with culture and history, and if you ever have the opportunity to experience this diamond in the rough, explore it as you will be pleasantly surprised.

Lesson: *If you want to know the truth, get up and find it for yourself.*

A Village Without Soul

I fell down the stairs of my house in the dumbest way, and I was alone! I was wearing plastic flip-flops while cleaning my house. The floor was marble and well-polished. Fortunately, I did fall from step three to the ground. The flip-flops slipped, and I lost my balance. I screamed as I rolled down the stairs. However, after waiting for a few minutes, no one heard my cry. There was only silence.

Coincidentally, I carried my cell phone in my pocket, which I never do when I am at home. It flew up in the air in the opposite direction to where I was lying on the floor. As I could, feeling pain in an arm and the lower part of the spine, coccyx area, I crawled like a baby and took the cell phone. I called the first four people on my contact list who live in the compound. Nobody answered. I waited and waited for 10 minutes or more, and no one responded. Without any response from my neighbors and lying on the floor, I decided to evaluate my current situation. I questioned myself: do you have any severe arm pain that could indicate a fracture? No. Do you have any severe pain in the lower part of the spine that could indicate a fracture? The answer was also No. Ok, Ana, I told myself, now you are going to move your arm, and you are going to try to get up. By the time that I got up from the floor, no one yet had responded to my phone messages. I got up; then, I noticed the bruise I had in my arm and the general hematomas I had on my back and legs.

Later in the week, the hematomas became purple, especially on the left buttock and on the arm. It looked like someone had beaten me! I did what I learned from my mom: ice cubes and Hirudoid (a magical topical lotion from Venezuela) that I carry with me everywhere, just in case of an accident.

The accident made me reflect on my personal story and the decisions that I had made. When one is older, experienced, divorced, independent, and on your own, one must accept the responsibilities of the life choices we make. Not having someone, as your companion, is a personal choice. You get older, and you fear that your freedom could be jeopardized by having another person near you. You are terrified by the only thought of the presence of another person who may be controlling your life, your personal space, and your day-to-day choices. You are even afraid of having someone as a partner, who would not understand your lifestyle, your autonomy, your liberty, and self-determination.

On the other hand, I thought about my health as I got older. What happens if I get sick? What happens if I have an accident and I break a leg or my hand? Those health-related questions as you age send you signals to be more careful when you walk, when you jump and when you want to do those things that you did perfectly well when you were younger. You realize that your mind is young, but your body does not respond anymore with the impetus of your savage spirit. Your body limits your interaction with your surroundings, and age starts imposing different modes of operation. Age does not forgive.

Falling down the stairs also made me reflect on the little sense of community that exists when living abroad. We transport our individualist culture, as it is in the Anglo culture. That social characteristic of culture is confronted by the collectivist nature of a culture such as the Arab or Latino ones. When I thought of the people I called, all of them were white Americans who never responded. It made me think about what would have happened if I had called one of my Arab neighbors instead. I am positive that someone would have been there for me immediately. An Arab would have come without qualms and would have helped me.

In the evening, when I went to bed, seeing myself with bruises and not having heard from any of my American colleagues, I thought, what would have happened if I had a head concussion or injury or a fracture? They could have found me two days later as they realized that I did not board the shuttle to go to the university.

It was possible that two days later, they could have found me dead or in critical condition. The accident was a wake-up call.

Lesson: Loneliness and age are not good companions.

"Tell your Daughter to Marry Another Time"

One of the most awkward moments in my life in the KSA was when I requested permission, academic leave for a week, to attend my daughter's destination wedding in the Dominican Republic.

At the beginning of the semester, after my 45-day summer vacation, I informed one of the university authorities, specifically the department chairperson, a Pakistani woman, that my daughter was getting married and that I planned to attend her destination wedding. She suggested I speak to the Dean of the college since the approval of a short leave of absence was out of her jurisdiction and authority.

I made an appointment to talk to the Dean, another Pakistani male expatriate, who had been in such a position for more than six years. He said, "I can't grant that leave of absence for the wedding of your daughter, and you must go to a higher academic authority to request that permission."

I followed his recommendation and went to see Dr. Mohammed. A male faculty, a national from Sudan, known for his bad temper and reputation for being rude, obstinate, discourteous, offensive, and impolite, particularly to female faculty. He had been in that position for more than 17-years. He was considered the gatekeeper of any faculty development and progress. He was the right hand of the Vice President of Academic Affairs. He could not do anything that would jeopardize his position of trust and confidence earned by violating the academic rights of faculty and staff.

Due to past and recent experiences with him, I knew that the situation ahead of me was not going to be easy. However, I had to face him. I need to handle the situation. If I wanted to attend my only daughter's wedding that had been planned for almost 18-months, I needed to confront him.

The day came for my meeting with him. I went to his office located between both campuses. I announced myself, and he did not lift his face. He ignored my presence. I insisted and said, "good morning." Then silence. I said again, good morning, and I did not get a response. I immediately realized that I was not welcome in the office. At that moment, I perceived that the circumstances of the meeting would not be the gratifying or an amicable one.

Suddenly, he said, "Who do you think you are?" And I responded, "Excuse me? Is that a question for me?"

"Yes," he said. "This institution takes teaching extremely serious, and family business has no place in the classroom." He continued, "The fact that you are a full professor, with high academic rank does not give you the right to take off because your daughter is getting married. Tell her to marry another time, not during the time her mother is working."

At that point, I had heard enough. I stood up and asked, "Is that what you would do if your daughter gets married while you are working?" At that very moment, as I angrily asked him, it occurred to me that in his culture, he makes those decisions and has control over his daughters – who to marry and when, including where and how the wedding celebration happens. That is not the case in the Western world.

I added, "I do not control my daughter's life events. She makes decisions on her own as an adult, she marries whoever she wants, and she plans the type of wedding that they both desire. I am going to my daughter's wedding, whether you like it or not. Watch me." I left.

Of course, I knew that I was going to be closely monitored from that very minute. Later in the week, my computer and my office calls were under surveillance every day. I was under scrutiny and close watch.

Lesson: You don't know how much you miss your own life until you are confronted with culturally irrational demands.

Breaking my Contract by
Escaping the Kingdom

I knew that I had to do something about attending my daughter's wedding in the fall. The senior administrator told me that my daughter needed to change her wedding date for another time while on vacation. Because I was teaching, in the middle of the academic semester, he would not permit me to attend my daughter's destination wedding planned two years before coming to Saudi.

I meditated and reflected on my options. The more I thought and analyzed, the closer I was to the fact that I was left without any choice but terminating my 2-year contract by escaping the Kingdom as many other people have done before for different reasons. But, how would I flee this restricted country? Who will be involved? Who to trust? When was the most appropriate date and time? What steps would I need to take to make my escape the least traumatic for my students and colleagues? What will I do with my furniture, kitchen utensils, bathroom rugs, decorations, paintings, pictures, among other things? There were tons of critical issues to consider before making the final decision. Then, what about my computer files? How do I purchase my airline ticket without using a computer and or without calling? Expatriates know that while in the Kingdom, your computers and phones are under surveillance. Trusting was a matter of life or death and telling someone about my plans would jeopardize my escape.

If you make an attempt to escape from the Kingdom, and it fails, the consequences are catastrophic. You would have to pay your contract in full, including the money that you already received. The university authorities retain your passport, and you are reported to the Ministry of Higher Education and the police. In Saudi, you must fear everybody. Not knowing who a government informant was, I needed to be extremely careful.

I thought about my driver. He must be the only person who I could trust. I did not have a choice. No. I was in his hands.

I called my driver and asked him to take me shopping. During the ride to the mall, I said, "Mr. Mohammed, I am leaving the country."

He asked, "Are you going on vacation, madame?" I said, "No, I am leaving the country for good." He responded, "So you are leaving at the end of the semester."
I replied," No, I am leaving in the next three weeks, by the end of this month." He turned his face suddenly, and with a pale face, he immediately warned me about the consequences of violating my contract. I said to him, "I want to trust you because you are the one helping me to escape." There was a silent moment.

I did not allow him to speak, and I explained what the situation was about my daughter's wedding and the denial of university administrators to grant a permit to be with my only daughter at that particular moment of her life.

He responded, "Dr. Ana, I will help you. When would you like to leave? Who else knows about this?" I said, "No one else but you." I asked him to keep pieces of my luggage at his home, which he agreed to do. For two consecutive Fridays, during the prayer time, he came and took my suitcases.

In the evenings, I placed some of my things in medium size bags and took them to one of my friends' home. I decided to inform my friend about the situation. She kept three of my boxes at her home, which months later, she brought to Manama (Bahrain) when I went back to spend the American Thanksgiving holiday to recover the rest of my belongings.

Little by little, I started emptying the golden cage, my home. Nobody knew what was going on inside. In terms of my university courses, classes resumed the third week of August. And before going back to class, I spent hours in my office deleting files from my computer. I tore documents, copied files, placed books in faculty mailboxes, (they did not know who did it). I organized folders with personal documents that I would need back in the States, among many other things to leave my office without any evidence or trace.

I took a risk and sent my daughter a text message using my cell phone from home and asked. Her to buy an airplane ticket leaving from Manama, and to pick me up at the airport. I also stated that she should please use a single word to indicate that it was done and the airline name. She followed the directions given. I knew that once I arrived at the airport, my ticket was going to be at the counter.

The day of my departure was set, and I invited three colleagues to spend the day in Manama to go and eat at a Mexican Restaurant that had music and margaritas. Only one of them knew about my fleeing the Kingdom. The other two accepted the trip as something that we would do when we wanted to breathe freely for a few hours. We needed to make my escape as a fun trip to Manama. Going to Manama on the weekends was the norm, not the exception. When we wanted to feel free of the limited environment imposed in the Kingdom, spending a day or weekend in Manama was an expedited solution. Going to Bahrain was always fun, but expensive. Usually, three women would pay one driver who stayed with us the entire day in Manana. He took us around to places and restaurants, including dancing clubs. For that reason, three women leaving for Bahrain would not call anyone's attention.

The morning of my departure arrived. The driver arrived with two of my colleagues. We stopped to pick the third one. They ignored that in the trunk of the car were my suitcases.

We started our road trip by giving Mohammed our passports. He was in charge of the operation. It is essential to explain that there is a bridge between Khobar (Saudi Arabia) and Manama (the capital city of the Sultanate of Bahrain). The King Fahd bin Abdulaziz Al Saud Causeway is a series of five bridges totaling 25 kilometers in length. The bridges connect Saudi and Bahrain. The Kingdom has three bridges, and Bahrain has two. There are three checkpoints between both countries. The driver is stopped three times to request passports and to open the trunk of the car to check suitcases or any other thing that the customs officials fear you are smuggling into the country. Often when returning from Bahrain to Saudi, some people try to bring alcohol.

Escaping from the Kingdom, breaking the contract is more routine than people think. International faculty are offered incentives and lucrative packages, however, the Saudi higher education administrators, do not honor their offers.

Contracts are "suggestions" of what your workload would be, your accommodations, your monthly salary represents, and many more misleading promises that are used by the international recruiters to buy your time in Saudi for at least one year. The university officials are accustomed to having faculty members leave without notice.

If you break your contract, you must pay back at least three months of your salary. Besides, there was nothing written about provisions for educational leaves related to family issues and emergencies. Educational or emergency leaves were decided by the male-dominated individual, the gatekeeper of the academic life of the institution. Those university officials remain in those job positions for a long time because they are incredibly loyal to the King, to the

University Rector, and their jobs. They are individuals with no life of their own.

We stopped at the first checkpoint. The driver said, "Do not look at the guards' faces. Behave normally, keep talking, and I'll take care of the passports." We followed his instructions. We drove to the second checkpoint from Saudi Arabia, and while still wearing our abayas, we were asked to step out of the car. We did and went inside the customs' main office. We used the facilities, bought water, acted normal, and we saw through the window when the officer asked the driver to open the trunk. At that moment, my body chilled. I did not know what excuses the driver provided to justify the suitcases in the trunk of his car. My colleagues felt the same. At that time, it was when the other two colleagues realized that something wasn't right. They both looked at me silently with an accomplished look. The driver walked toward us and said, "Let's go. You are going to miss your flights!" When I heard the plural use of the noun "flight," I did not ask any questions because I realized he was covering for me. I immediately figured out.

We drove to the last checkpoint; he paid the fee for us and continued driving. We waited for ten minutes, and when we were sure that we had reached Bahrain territory, we took our *abayas* off, we uncovered our heads, and we all said harmoniously, "Yes, we did it!" We laughed nervously. We wanted to yell and scream.

Before taking me to the airport, we had lunch together, drank and danced! By 5.00 pm, the time came to say goodbye. I cannot say that it was painless. No, it was hard, painful, disturbing, uncomfortable, and heart-breaking. I was leaving behind another chapter of my life: my professional life.

Most importantly, I was leaving behind a group of human beings who formed my new family while I lived there. People who became part of my stories, my new narratives. Women with hopes and dreams.

The movie of my 400 days in Saudi passed in a minute, and I characterized them as challenging, interesting, exhilarating, and unforgettable. My friends did not want to say goodbye. There was an underlying agreement on not turning our faces back and keep walking as if we were going to see each other the next day. I prayed for them internally. There is one good thing about KSA: the great feeling of joy once you are sitting on the plane going back home!

Lesson: When you have left without choices, your life experiences are transformed into your internal voices of wisdom.

Memorandum of Understanding

As an expatriate, I met people from all walks of life.

I met this mysterious faculty woman who became an enigma for many. We did not know how to read her. She was quiet, distracted, unapproachable, and puzzled. She was contracted from America to be the Chair of a business-related department. Although she preserved her enigmatic posture, it took her two months to open up a little bit, to smile more on the bus, and to invite another person to sit next to her while riding to the main campus.

I soon learned how to deal with her. She wanted to portray herself as very academic, a strict researcher, and a prolific presenter before arriving in Saudi. She came to my home three times for different reasons: an invitation for breakfast, Eastern lunch, and signing a memorandum of understanding for a possible book we planned to work on together. The memorandum of understanding said: "Let it be known that this is an agreement between Dr. ET and Dr. Ana Gil Garcia. The agreement is that both parties are collaborating to write a pocketbook with the working title: *Under the Abaya*, which is a descriptive account of academic, professional, and cultural life in Saudi Arabia using the alphabet (A to Z words). The project began in May 2015. Both parties are in agreement to continue sharing the role of contributing to the content, writing, promotion, and any all proceeds generated by this book project. Both parties share all copyrights to this project."

We met two Saturdays in the beautiful kitchen of my golden cage to work on the A to Z outline of the book. After brainstorming the glossary and organizing it, she suddenly disappeared. Some colleagues said that she was ill and asked for a medical leave. Other people said that she was terminated. And others referred to another one of the usual escapes from the unsatisfied job. The truth of the matter is that my potential co-author, who asked me to officialize what I thought was an unofficial and cordial talk, through a memorandum of understanding the publication of a book, was nowhere to be found. I am writing this book that intentionally is different from the MOU description. Hopefully, she will read it to realize that we can still write the A to Z Under the Abaya narrative pocketbook.

Lesson: You respect the agreements, even if they are on dead letter

Passing for Arab in an Arab Nation

Being racially ambiguous has its advantages and disadvantages in the Kingdom. For the most part, Saudi's thought I was one of them, or at least Arab.

When I went shopping, the store clerks would greet me in Arabic. When I was in the markets bartering, they would usually give me the local prices. My students could not accept that I was a 'Westerner' and that my facial features and skin tone justified my Arab origins. I was one of them, and that meant everything to them. It meant that students felt more comfortable to speak with me about their private affairs because they believed that I could relate.

For my suitors, it meant that I was someone that they could bring home to their families and potentially introduce me as the woman they wish to marry. It said that I gained a cultural 'pass.' Access to Saudi circles and their way of life. It also meant that I was expected to behave like a good Arab/Muslim woman. I must distinguish the difference. Not all Arabs are Muslim, and not all Muslims are Arabs. However, in this case, at first glance, I was identified as being both. On many occasions, I was reprimanded by the religious police, known as the *mutawa* for not wearing my headscarf and that as an Arab Muslim woman, I should be setting an example. When I tried to tell him that I was a Westerner and not Arab, he laughed and told me to 'never let it happen again.' Sometimes camouflaging into a society can backfire and can cause a lot of problems. Passing for an Arab can get you into trouble when you're trying to visit friends in Western compounds.

There are usually two or three checkpoints to gain access to a compound, and it depends on the level of security that is in place and the personnel it houses. When you look Arab, be prepared to be scrutinized, because Saudi's are not supposed to be on compounds for Westerners.

Once you have proven, you are a 'Westerner,' you gained access and enjoyed the compound lifestyle.

When my friends took me to the American military compounds to meet guys, many of them were hesitant in speaking with me because they assumed that I was an Arab, looking for an alcoholic fix and curious about the expat lifestyle. It was only after a few drinks that they would warm up to me and discover my North American roots. I was one of them, and there was no need to "figure me out." I said that having the privilege to access both worlds served as a huge advantage. I was able to assimilate and live like an Arab, while also living like an expat. There are not many people that get the opportunity to experience that.

Lesson: As my mother would always say; one day, you will appreciate all of the features that make you unique. They will serve you along your path.

Educational Environment

By definition, an educational environment refers to the diverse physical locations, contexts, and cultures in which students learn what teachers teach.

In this second chapter on the educational environment, we will take you to a different dimension of learning and teaching. The setting is explored from the perspectives of factual events that took place in and out of the classroom but in the premises of the university walls. The incidents occurred in a non-coed climate in which female students are the only protagonists of the stories. Due to the legal and enforced regulations of the higher education institution where the stories took place, it is essential to clarify that female faculty cannot teach male students. For that reason, what you will read in the educational learning environment will relate to the feminine side of any academic story.

This chapter analyzes teaching modalities and assessment practices that, when implemented appropriately, drive student achievement. The stories of the use of mobile phones in the classroom for different purposes, such as increasing access to innovative content, navigating the internet for learning, and misusing mobiles for cheating, bribery, and plagiarism, are the platform for analysis.

The higher education environment is permeated by factual events experienced by the authors while teaching undergraduate female students from different disciplines. The chapter includes an analysis of the teaching contract signed before arrival and the revision of it after arrival that, we hope, would support other colleagues with the right intention to teach in the Kingdom.

The academic load may involve different cultural meanings for expatriate faculty and the local ones. If your academic rank is higher, you should teach twelve credit hours. However, the purpose of twelve credit hours in an American classroom could be three courses of four credits or four courses of three credit hours. In Saudi, the teaching load reflects the number of credit hours per class; it is to say, one credit per course. The discrepancy between both systems is relevant. So, you may be forced to teach twelve courses since your academic rank indicates a maximum of twelve credit hours!

Class sizes, academic commitment designations, the use of small groups as a traditional methodology of work and interaction, research challenges, educational benefits, and academic freedom are stories that the concerned faculty have as they decide to teach in the Kingdom of Saudi Arabia.

Misunderstanding Teaching Load

The next day after my arrival in Saudi, I visited the campus. I wanted to learn more about my teaching load, my administrative duties, time for research, the kind of academic services to be provided to the institution, working conditions, and practices, among other educational aspects of my immediate academic life in a Saudi institution.

Very early in the morning, I took the first shuttle from the compound to the university. I realized immediately that the campus was far, almost outside the city and that for a faculty teaching at 8:00 am, he/she should be in the earliest bus shift. It took the bus approximately one hour to arrive at the campus. I noticed the people that took the shuttle the earliest. The majority of the early birds were staff members and janitors. I also noticed that they were Filipinos, who I later learned were contracted not only by educational institutions but also by Saudi families who hired them to serve as domestic workers.

During my time on the bus, I observed the physical environment. I noticed the calm waters of the sea along the way and some isolated big houses that looked like hallucinations in the middle of the desert. I jumped off the bus that usually stopped in the back of the female campus and went inside.

I asked for the location of the Department of Humanities, and someone directed me there. I met my chairperson, and after exchanging introductions and a summary of my trip, she kindly walked me to my office. At my office, I asked her about my teaching load, syllabus, and assessment practices. She showed me a list of ten courses. She said, "This is the list of the courses you will be teaching."

I replied, "I think that there is a mistake, there are ten courses, and I am expected to teach twelve credit hours only."

She replied, "Yes, in fact, there are twelve hours here for you to teach. Your teaching load is made up of eight courses of one credit hour and two courses of two credit hours each." I thought that I was going to die. Unfortunately, I was operating with my western mentality in which a faculty of my academic rank cannot teach more than three courses of three credit hours each. Not in Saudi institutions.

The curriculum consists of hundreds of courses of only one or two credit hours. It never occurred to me to ask how many courses constituted a workload for a full professor before deciding on teaching in a Saudi institution of higher education. A big mistake that I regretted later!

Lesson: Read the small print of your education contract and avoid misunderstandings that could be transformed into major mental health issues later.

False Medical Report to Justify School Absenteeism

In Saudi universities, taking attendance is a practice from high school that has not been abolished. Every day the instructor takes attendance and keeps track of who is in the classroom. The system has created rules and regulations, such as withdrawing students from class after missing 5%, 10%, and 15% of class sessions.

Taking attendance is one more administrative function regardless if the faculty is already teaching more than five courses. The instructor sends a warning letter informing about 5% of absenteeism after the first two weeks of the starting date of the semester. Two weeks later, another warning letter is sent in which faculty reports to the students the number of classes they have missed. A final letter is sent halfway into the semester, warning the student that she will be removed from the class roster due to more than 15% of absences.

When students reach that point, they look for different ways to justify the absences to avoid being dropped from the course by the instructor. One of the most common practices is to bring medical reports describing a doctor's visit and any other type of medical procedure. The students know that only a medical report would validate and excuse their absences.

In a private conversation with some of them, they confirmed that some medical centers specialize in fabricating false medical reports. They sell them not only to students but anyone who needs to give a good reason for missing a day (or many) of work or, in this case, a class session. Of course, all rules have exceptions. Not all students manufacture a medical excuse. Some are serious about their school attendance and the importance of being physically present in the classroom. Through those rules about absenteeism, the Saudi university system has created a corrupted culture that is known by high administrators and faculty.

In our opinion, making students responsible for their academic behavior, such as attendance, would support a healthy educational environment in which lies, and false testimonies would be minimized.

Lesson: The more punitively complex a system becomes, the less respect and consideration for values and ethical behaviors.

A Lucrative Business –
Plagiarism and Cheating

The concepts of cheating and plagiarism seem to be unknown in Saudi Arabia. The collectivist structure of the tribal society perceives cheating as an act of collaboration and brotherhood.

In the classroom, female students use several resources to cheat, especially technological devices. The faculty talk about, tell stories, laugh on, but overall try to understand the frequency and general use of cheating in the classroom. It is common practice to bribe faculty with weekend travels (all-inclusive), exquisite pieces of jewelry, expensive dinners, even gross sums of money.

Plagiarism is a business. A paper costs $300 to $3000! The assignments have a sticker price depending on the number of pages and the subject that needs to be researched. Outside university walls, there are individuals whose business is to write papers for the female students.

In my two academic semesters, not less than 75% of my students plagiarized their papers. Their attitude toward a professional career that they may use in the future might contribute to the disengagement from their motivation to learn.

The first written assignment I read, from three sections of Leadership and Teamwork courses, shocked me. I read the first paper, used my assessment rubric, and gave a grade. As I read the second paper, it seemed to me that I had read it before. When I opened the previous paper, every paragraph of both papers was identical. I decided to select assignments from the other two sections randomly, and surprisingly, I found exact papers, not even a comma changed, among twenty-three papers!

As a professor, I needed to make a decision: every student will receive a zero score or a full score. My colleagues could not understand my rationale to give them full credit, although they plagiarized their papers.

When I raised questions about curriculum changes in the university since its foundation seven years ago, I was told that faculty members were not allowed to make any curriculum changes in the syllabus. Renewal of content, book selection, revision of assessments, teaching delivery techniques, technology infusion, among other aspects of the classroom plan could not be modified or adjusted. Even more, faculty was punished if they introduced any minor changes in the way of presenting their course content.

Based on this toxic academic measure that still promotes clear violations of academic freedom, every semester, faculty was severely enforced to use and repeat the same instructional materials that brought significant consequences such as recycling assignments by students.

I opted to give the students full points because the university's policies did not punish students for plagiarism or cheating: two major detractors of education and knowledge.

The imposition of a culture of plagiarism and cheating is encouraged and endorsed by the university curriculum rules and policies.

Female students are the victims of a culture that sponsors unethical behaviors and misrepresentations of integrity and honesty. In my opinion, the students act the way they do, because the academic system has infused and injected wrong doses of dishonest and dishonorable conduct.

Lesson: Students cannot be penalized or punished by policies that favor wrongdoings.

My Work is Not Yours!

Two students in one of my leadership & teamwork classes submitted a paper that did not belong to them. It was an act of plagiarism. However, this one was very peculiar because the paper that was plagiarized belonged to me, the instructor of the class! One of my papers was copied from the internet by someone who writes essays for female students for money.

Plagiarism, cheating, and any form of unethical behavior are a common practice in many classrooms in Saudi Arabia. How dumb could you be not to realize that your instructor originally wrote the paper submitted? Two things crossed my mind. First, it was apparent they did not read the paper before submitting it, and secondly, they did not write the paper that was submitted.

It took me only one minute to verify that the paper I was reading was from my academic production. My initial reaction was to laugh. Right after, I reflected upon the academic integrity and student code of conduct. Are they enforced? Living and teaching here for one year provided me with the strong evidence that those unethical behaviors were not penalized. The enforcement of the Student Code of Conduct does not take place for many reasons: misunderstanding of compassion, bribery, faculty fear, lack of academic freedom, administration interference, and unwillingness to be signaled by the higher administration as a rude uncooperative faculty.

The students that plagiarized my work were not reprimanded. I informed the department Chair and showed her evidence of the plagiarism. Nevertheless, she laughed about the situation and requested a second chance for the students.

In any other country, both students would have been expelled automatically. Not in Saudi Arabia. Not enforcing codes of conduct is an invitation for students to continue abusing and disrespecting faculty and violating the education they are receiving.

Lesson: *Reinforcing ethical behaviors must be the educational norm; it should not be perceived as an exception to the rule.*

My Daughter's Grade

Many faculty and administrators in Saudi have their children attending the universities where they work and teach. Similar to other countries, most higher education institutions include the exemption and waiver of registration and enrollment fees as one of the faculty personnel benefits and perks for their family members. However, unlike other countries, on occasion, faculty receive phone calls from top administration managers asking for their daughters' final grades. Without any reservation nor shame, the administrators demand higher grades for their children. Also, the rumor was that they had access to making grade changes if the grade of their children was not as what they expected.

I struggled with believing that rumor until it knocked on my door. Two days before the final exam of one of the courses I teach Leadership & Teamwork, the father of one of my students called me directly from his office on campus. The conversation went like this: "Good morning, Dr. Ana (no last names are used in the Middle East countries for professors with a doctorate), how are you? What do you think about the meeting that we had two days ago about research grants? I responded to what I was asked, and immediately after, he said, "Do you know that my daughter is in your Leadership and Teamwork class?"

I responded, "Yes, I know. I asked her if she was related to you because of her last name, and she said that she was your daughter."

The Vice-President asked, "How is she doing in your class? What type of grade will she get? Will she get more than a B?" When he said that, I was not sure if I heard correctly.

I replied, "So far, she has a B; once she takes her final exam, she will have the final grade she earns…"

Forty years in the business of education, and I had not heard that request ever. I learned that there is always a first time in life and that every day you learn something new. His daughter earned a B+ in my class.

Lesson: There is always a first time in your educational journey that teach you something new.

The Exchange of an Exquisite Perfume

A week before the final week and the final submission of the leading research paper of a Writing & Research course I taught, an 18-year old undergraduate student invited me to have dinner with her and her grandmother. Surprisingly, she asked for my food preferences. I praised the generosity and kindness of the Arab culture, and I gladly accepted.

We met at a seafood restaurant in downtown Khobar. As soon as we arrived in the Family Section of the restaurant, in which only females and families are allowed, my young and pretty student uncovered her head and put on the table, her research paper. She then said, "Here is my research paper, and I would like you to read it before eating so that I can get an A in your class." I was in shock. I thought our time together was going to be a pleasant evening learning about family traditions, social culture, protocol competences, and food introduction. Instead, it resulted in being a "set up" dinner in which I was expected to grade a paper, provide my academic feedback, and commit to an A grade on her research paper.

Without the opportunity to respond, her grandmother placed a small bag with two perfumes on the table. She said, "My daughter cries every day because she says that your class is very hard. I would like you to give my granddaughter an A grade. We can pay you to teach her privately."

I replied, "I am very sorry, but I do not teach private lessons to my students. There is a conflict of interest. If I do that for one student, I have to do it for all."

Her granddaughter replied, "Dr. Ana, no one will know. I will not tell anyone that you read my paper or that you will teach me before the final test."

Unexpectedly, my dinner became bribery for an A grade. The mental movie of my academic life quickly took me to my many years in higher education classrooms, dealing with undergraduate and graduate students from different backgrounds, nationalities, religions, gender, and values. Yet, nothing like it.

My brain sent messages to my stomach, and what was expected to be an incredible seafood dinner was ultimately ruined.

Lesson: Values and ethical behaviors are stronger than tangible temporary rewards.

A Bribery with Cartier

Teaching at a private university with a bunch of rich kids can be quite an experience.

I taught ESL to an elite group of female Saudi students that did not hesitate to come to class decked out in the latest runway trends. The majority of my students had Rolexes around their wrists, Chanel wallet on chain bags, and the signature Hermes sandals. They would top their look with heavy contoured makeup, fully filled-in signature "Saudi eyebrows," and a few spritzes of the highest quality Oud perfume. These girls were not afraid to demonstrate their wealth in the classroom, and they made sure to let their teachers know of their wealth during exam week.

Exam week was stressful enough. There were glitches with computers and Wi-Fi connections, student's orchestrating inventive ways to cheat on their assessments, and long days of proctoring and conducting exam protocols.

Once exams finished, teachers would have a week to mark and enter the final grades into the system. This week was called "Bribery week." Students would trickle into your office and negotiate their grades with you by offering you food, expensive gifts, and in some cases, money.

I knew a teacher who turned bribery into a lucrative side hustle. She established a price system for the letter grade a student desired! Eventually, the administration caught on to her shenanigans, and they sent her back to her native country, like a one suitcase woman.

I, on the other hand, was bribed with a lovely Cartier bracelet and earring set. The student came into my office and closed the door quietly behind her. She took a seat and began to compliment me, telling me that she really enjoyed my class and that she was going to miss me as a teacher. Saudi female students are sneaky. I knew where she was going with this, but I allowed her to carry on. She began to shed crocodile tears and stated that she had failed the course two times prior and that her father would be distraught if there were a third time. She continued to plead and justify her lack of enthusiasm all semester and asked me to increase her grade to a pass. In exchange, she placed a dark blue velvet jewelry box on my desk and said, "I want to give you this present miss." I took the box and opened to see what was inside. It was a beautiful gold and diamond-encrusted Cartier bracelet and matching earrings. "Do you like it, Miss?" I told her that it was beautiful and must have cost a pretty penny. She smiled and said, "I chose it just for you."

I replied, "Thank you for the gesture, but I have to ask…if I take this gift, are you expecting me to increase your grade?" She paused and smirked. I told her that if she wanted me to have this gift, she should come back when the semester is finished, and I am no longer her teacher, and I will gladly accept the gift.

She smiled and retrieved the velvet box and placed it in her bag. "Ok, miss, thank you." I nodded my head with acknowledgment, and she swiftly left my office. That was the last time I saw that student. She never did return to give me that beautiful Cartier bracelet and earring set.

Lesson: Free cheese is always available in mouse traps.

Committee Appointments

When you are the high academic rank faculty member on campus, you are appointed to most committees that regulate the academic life of the university. That was my case. It became the norm to receive committee appointments directly from the president, provost, and Dean without asking for your desires about those committees.

They assumed that my high academic rank on the female campus made me the appropriate faculty to be a member of several committees. I was expected to participate in the curriculum committee, professional development committee, graduate research committee, academic advising committee, organizational culture, and climate committee, and more because the high-level university authorities believed that I could provide guidance and expertise. I could not refuse to belong to a committee. It was considered my duty and obligation. Besides, I couldn't decline an appointment from the President or Provost without being considered rude and disrespectful. It is not about my expertise in the field, but about obedience to the top leaders of the institution. I was not to question the authority; even more, as a female, I was forced to abide by the authority rules and procedures of a male administrator. I sent an email to the Dean of the College of Humanities with my reasons explaining why I did not want to work in the four committee appointments, and I soon learned when he emailed back that I did not have a choice. It was my duty only to accept mandates.

My schedule was now from 7:00 am to 4:00 pm every day, with no breaks or rest. I had to admit that my mood changed, my anxiety level topped the ceiling, and my frustration with the administration was increased.

Lesson: Learning to say no is a process that must be put into practice in a male dominated education environment.

The Class Size Menace

One of the most challenging situations for me, while in the Kingdom, was class size combined with teaching load.

I had to teach ten courses with 30-35 freshman females in each, which meant teaching 300 to 350 students weekly. Even if I wanted to learn their names, for example, it was an impossible task.

I wanted to do my best to teach them an assessment, academic writing, research, and leadership. However, the educational reality was forcing me to spend fifteen minutes checking attendance, ten minutes disciplining students, and ten minutes verifying whether the students had completed their assignments.

By the end of class, I only had ten minutes for new curriculum content. I taught from 8:00 am to 4:00 pm every day. That implied teaching five to six classes daily. In a day, I easily taught 150 to 200 students. It was probably perceived as an acceptable academic workload to be performed by a lower-ranked instructor.

Nevertheless, any seasoned faculty would teach no more than fifteen to twenty students daily. I regret not having done a much better job teaching at the highest level of excellence with different delivery methods and technology practices. Yet, the existing job conditions refrained me from doing so. I could have given more, but due to the class size and expectations, I was unable to.

The students realized my inability to teach them adequately with so many classes. They challenged me in many ways; academically, culturally, socially, and administratively.

They were aware of my academic weaknesses in dealing with all non-English speaking students, and they took advantage. I spent hours speaking basic academic vocabulary to ensure that all of them would comprehend the meaning and significance of the theme studied. Although I did my best in teaching English language learners, the curriculum content suffered the consequences of large class sizes.

Lesson: To understand an educator's journey, one must learn to navigate the waters of the teaching conditions.

Setting up Small Group

One of the most significant challenges in the classroom was setting up small and fully functional groups.

Groups allow students to work together, interact, and discuss assignments to equip them to become responsible for their academic performance during an academic semester. At the educational institution in the Kingdom, it was almost an impossible task.

Female students have their favorite people that they wanted to work with. Regardless of an introductory presentation of each person before forming the small group, the female students refused openly to work with one or another person. They frankly did not care about offending others, about not wanting them to be members of their groups. They did not show any shame in excluding someone without an explanation, and the word 'courtesy' did not exist as they were forming groups.

Since the classes were large, with more than thirty students, each small group was made up of five or six members. The situation became so intolerant that groups of only three people were created. They intentionally ignored the classroom rules about the number of members for each of the groups. Some students argued about the distance from their towns and the university in the event they had to work together outside the classroom. I thought it was a valid argument. Another argument was that they studied together in the private high school they attended, and they knew how to work together as a group. This was not a valid argument. Another argument was more elitist and classist. The university has low-income students that benefit from donors to attend the university. However, high-class students did not want to mingle and mix with lower-class students.

As I made my final decision, I experienced the consequences. The Dean and the Chairperson called me to reconsider the small group arrangements in my class for the sake and benefit of the students. They alleged, "student first." I immediately understood that anything that happened in class; the students would complain to the highest authority. This reminded me of the questionable academic freedom and the lack of professionalism of high-ranking administrators. They imposed what students could get away with, instead of focusing on the benefits of the instructional strategy of grouping for the dynamic of the class.

Lesson: The violation of your academic freedom depends on the demands of the ruler.

The Power of Academic Meetings
to Improve Gender Relations

Globally, universities and colleges demand from their faculty members to serve on committees for the educational benefits of the institution. The university in Khobar was not different, except that I was the only female attending high administrative level meetings. The university mission had three pillars: teaching, research, and service. The latter, service, includes being a member of two to three committees during a semester, especially if the faculty is on a tenure-track position. There are diverse kinds of meetings. Among them, academic, administrative, social, sport, and governance. The academic meetings at the institutional level that I participated in were related to academic affairs, personnel issues, graduation requirements, student services, research policies, and graduate affairs.

At the departmental level, I chaired the curriculum committee, research committee, personnel issues, and newsletter advisor. My academic rank determined my appointment in as many committees as anyone in a higher education institution would convene to be part of. I was expected to comply with a teaching load of ten courses weekly. I served in five institutional committees, and four departmental committees, and I managed to stay sane!

Being the only female in an institutional committee implied that my voice was ignored, and the decisions made did not consider my professional opinion on the academic issue being discussed and analyzed. While I believe in adjusting cultural competencies to specific organizational culture and climate, it is also true that there are conflicts and clashes between Western and Middle Eastern administrative practices.

The dynamic of the meetings changed according to who was present. If the Provost or Vice President of Academic Affairs attended the meeting, then he was the only person who could talk, say, rule, discuss and decide. No one was allowed to reply or provide any opinions. When males were in the room, think about the role of the woman at the meeting. My presence was overlooked, unnoticed, and passed over.

Although I was an experienced faculty with many years of work in and out of the classrooms, I usually observed before emitting my opinion. I avoided speaking at the first two meetings unless I was asked for my opinion.

I remember being part of the discussion on personnel issues such as tenure, promotion, and or other forms of faculty advancement. With more than fifteen years of experience working as a chair of the departmental personnel committee, my opinion had no value added to that exchange. I made two attempts to be heard, but nothing seemed to indicate their intentions of allowing me to speak. As the group of male faculty was ready to vote on the issue, I abstained. The look on faces, especially from the Vice President of the institution, was evident that he heard me correctly. I again indicated that I abstained and that it had to be recorded on the minutes.

The university was under an evaluation process, and the accrediting agency carefully examined all meeting agendas and minutes. Internal chaos occurred in the meeting, and many hands were agitated. In the end, they asked me to explain my vote, which I did. From that moment, I spoke, and they listened. My professional opinion was considered, and regardless of the high-rank position they held, they understood that a female voice has equal value, especially if it comes from a seasoned faculty with diversified expertise.

Lesson: Have a high opinion of yourself, know who you are and what you stand for and demand respect.

The Violation of a Contract

Faculty who accept to come to Saudi universities are tied up for a month or two until they receive their national identification or *Iqama*.

During that time, your passport is confiscated, and that is when you learn the meaning of your contract, the one you signed before you left your home country, and the one the university requires you to sign upon your arrival.

In my employment contract, it indicated that "The Employer will appoint the Employee as a Full Professor in Humanities and Social Sciences, Core Program." In another point in the contract, it says: "Faculty workloads and teaching assignments are determined by the Dean. In general, the workloads will vary by the rank of the appointment." Both parts of my contract explicitly indicated that my workload was according to my academic rank of full professor. That was a misrepresentation of the truth.

Since most universities lately created in the Kingdom want to emulate American universities, it is still far from what you can expect. There are no similarities. The differences are severely profound. In comparison, a full professor in United States institutions of higher education teaches a maximum of four courses of three or four credit hours each. The general teaching load of a full time, full professor is twelve credit hours that might represent three classes. In Saudi, twelve credit hours are ten or twelve courses. Most courses are of one or two credit hours.

When I read the contract, it claimed that I would be teaching according to my academic rank and, unfortunately, I assumed that implied three or four courses, not twelve. The Saudi administrators surprised me with ten to twelve courses inferring that they did not lie or mislead me. What happened, they said, was that I did not ask the right questions.

The contract also spelled out, that as a full academic rank professor, I was expected to be engaged in teaching, research/scholarship, and service.

I am warning you - be careful of what you read and comprehend. If you are a research-oriented faculty and you are a woman, be aware that you will be limited to research that you would be able to deliver in and or out of the Kingdom borders. As a researcher, I was denied three times to attend international conferences to deliver my research studies. I submitted on time the proper requirements, completed my university forms, attached the complete paper, and an acceptance letter from the conference committees, and processed all documentation on time. However, the Academic Affairs Office denied my conference participation without any explanation.

It is essential to clarify that the contract indicates that "Research and academic activities have a considerable weight in the faculty assessment process and in the provisions of faculty renewal for faculty members. Faculty members are expected to attend conferences, to publish a minimum of one research paper annually in a high impact journal...". Once on-site, the contract became a worthless piece of paper.

At my interview for the position, the academic and administrative officials made me believe that the current educational conditions were transferable to the new education environment I was about to face.

It is also relevant to mention that the contract that I signed referred to my behavior and conduct in accordance with the generally accepted customs of my profession. It stated that I would abide by the laws, policies, regulations, and TRADITIONS of the Kingdom of Saudi Arabia as long as I was an employee in the Kingdom. The employee, the contract said, would undertake the responsibility for any violation of these laws and regulations. The agreement reinforced that employees are subject to all laws of the KSA as well as the rules of the Employer. What the contract did not say was that I could be penalized in Saudi even for misunderstanding the culture. It is to say; you may end up in jail or be lashed out in public for committing a crime that may not be a crime in the eyes of an expatriate — for example, public dating expressions.

The myth of the high salary is amply advertised as the hook for recruiting foreign academicians. Far from the truth is the fact that a full professor makes the same salary as in America. For example, the academic rank of full professor makes twenty-two thousand one hundred and thirty-eight Saudi Riyals ($5,903) monthly. A total of $70,800 annually. The contract indicates that the "Employee shall bear all taxes, fees, allowances, and penalties payable by him/her in accordance with the laws in force in Saudi Arabia." Although there are some perks as, for example, rental of your accommodation and or a bonus for transportation, the maximum salary could reach $75,000. A full professor at any state university or community college in the United States would make a higher salary annually than the one offered in Saudi. In reality, negotiations work better for men. The male-dominated environment believes that males deserve to be paid higher wages than females regardless of their academic rank and seniority. What is true is that if you are a US citizen, you may have tax exemption only if you have stayed 335 days in foreign lands in one fiscal year. If you come to visit your family, be aware that the limit of your vacation is 30 days if you want to take advantage of the taxation system for foreigners.

Lesson: Always read the small print, ask questions for clarification purposes, do not make any assumptions about any word in the contract, and do not sign documents that might put you in trouble culturally.

The Challenge of Researching
Forbidden Topics

In Saudi Arabia, teaching research to first-year students was challenging.

One time, one of my students came to my office to discuss her potential research project. She said, so naively, that she would like to research on sexual orientation and gay marriage in Saudi Arabia. I asked her twice to repeat what she said; I almost fell off my chair! I questioned her about the legal restrictions and religion constraints in her culture. She said, "I am aware of those limitations, but I know many gays and lesbians who dream to live with their partners freely." She expanded by saying that Saudi men having sex with other men do not consider themselves gays; the same-sex relationship happens to fulfill a need, but it is not an individual identity. She also said that being gay is easier than being straight in Saudi. For example, as a female, if she went out with a boy, then she would be questioned by people and or the moral police, and that would not happen if accompanied by another female.

After discouraging her not to conduct a research study that could jeopardize both of us, I looked up information on the legal aspects related to LGBT in Middle Eastern countries. It did not surprise me at all that Saudi Arabia is one of six Arab countries that claim *Sharia* (Islamic law) as its legal code. The Sharia law makes the Kingdom of Saudi Arabia the least tolerant of gay and lesbian behaviors in the GCC region. Under this legal framework, sex outside marriage is illegal.

As same-sex marriage is not permitted, same-sex intimacy is a crime. The punishment varies from the death penalty to flogging. I am not sure if the response given by my research student was a "set-up" for me as a foreigner or if she was indeed aware of the information she provided. I used my keen and experienced instincts and asked her not to research an issue that was difficult to study under the social, cultural, and legal conditions of the country. I asked her to think about a more suitable and researchable topic in which data would be more accessible to analyze.

Lesson: Read between the lines and let your personal and professional experiences guide you.

Academic Freedom as a Foreign Concept

The concept of academic freedom is a foreign one at most Saudi universities.

The Ministry of Higher Education rules every aspect of the academic life of colleges and universities, including the number of weeks per semester, institutional academic calendar, holidays, and hiring procedures, among others.

Private universities may enforce additional rules and regulations to preserve their doors open. They differ remarkably from Western institutions in terms of the number of weeks in the academic semester. The institutions impose nineteen weeks instead of fifteen; the final exam weeks are excluded because final exams are not considered instructional weeks.

The interventionist frame used by some private universities creates an unbearable violation of academic freedom. The instructional technology platforms such as Blackboard and D2L are investigated to verify whether or not a faculty has input the students' grades or has complied with the use of assessment rubrics to evaluate students' written assignments.

In a higher education classroom, faculty must provide a progress attendance report that includes writing down the number of absences of a student to warn the adult student about her potential of being withdrawn from the course due to 5 or 10% of absences. Faculty are forced to maintain records of medical reports, usually fake justifications paid by students to unscrupulous medical doctors. A faculty has no freedom in selecting the course textbooks. A faculty lacks the freedom to choose the type of assessment and teaching techniques. A faculty cannot infuse any curriculum innovation in class without the fear of being penalized by the top administrators. As a seasoned faculty, I appreciate more and more the academic freedom that we still enjoy in higher education classrooms in the western hemisphere. As a university faculty who previously experienced academic freedom, I was unaware of how much I missed that freedom. One day I received an email from the Dean of the College of Core Humanities informing me about the result of the investigation of my Blackboard activities, grades, announcements, and emails I sent to general and to individual students. I could not believe what I read in the email message!

Academic restrictions and violations of your academic integrity make you wonder how much longer a principled faculty working in Saudi Arabia can resist the maximum violation of the sanctuary for teaching and learning in the classroom.

Lesson: The rights in your own cultural context can be used as a basis for understanding the restrictions of another environment.

The Perks and Benefits of a Golden Cage

The university system in Saudi is exceptionally respectful of academic ranks and longevity.

The higher the academic status, the more respect you receive and the most prestige the institution has. When I arrived in Saudi as a teaching professional, I ignored that my academic rank would provide me with some benefits that I would not enjoy back home. For example, as a full professor, I lived with the institution high-rank administrators such as department heads, Deans, and Vice-Presidents. The compound (housing facilities) for the administrators was smaller than any other housing facility due to its exclusiveness of the type of residents living in it, and the individual houses were more luxurious.

My designated home was a small mansion, as I used to call it. It had two floors, four bedrooms with private bathrooms, two living rooms, a dining room, a TV room, a laundry room, and a large Italian kitchen fully equipped. The house was fully equipped and furnished with brand new furniture; I took off the sale tags of the furniture! The kitchen utensils were of high quality. I had a unique private office that invited me to work, read, and write. I had this small mansion for myself, a single person, and it was overwhelming.

After my arrival, I had a meeting with the academic officer for induction purposes. During our conversation, I brought up my massive living space since I was just one person. He immediately replied: Don't you like your accommodations? I let him know my satisfaction with the residence assigned to me, but at the same time, I expressed my opinion on the exaggerated dimensions of the house for only one person. At that meeting, I learned that because of my high academic rank professorship on the female campus, my housing was different from any other expatriate female instructor. My house was a golden cage. However, it also was my refuge.

Soon enough, I figured out my routine for doing laundry, cleaning both floors, cooking, watching TV, and reading and grading papers.

Every day the university bus dropped me off at my door. I opened my door, walked directly to the kitchen, warmed up some food, previously cooked on weekends, and then I sat in a comfortable chair in the family TV room to watch the news while eating my dinner. Immediately after eating, I took a nap while watching TV. The level of exhaustion was overwhelming. In America, I never napped.
In Saudi, my body learned to crash after dealing with 250 students daily!

On Fridays, while the entire city was praying in the mosques, I was doing laundry and cleaning before prayers were over. The house chores ended by 3:00 pm. By then, I had reserved a car to take me food shopping, do my manicure, pedicure, and massages. Before I even blinked, the day was gone!

Lesson: Learn to enjoy what you have earned in life.

Culture Bashing in Academia

In the ESL Program at the university, we would hold regular professional development workshops.

Instructors who attended a series of workshops offered throughout the academic school year are awarded a Certificate of Professional Development.

I attended a workshop that focused on literacy strategies for Saudi students. I thought that it would be an excellent opportunity to learn methodologies that I could incorporate to help my students become more enthusiastic about reading in the ESL classroom. The person who led the workshop was a white, middle-aged American expat, who had a reputation for being obnoxious and ignorant. I tried to give him the benefit of the doubt and thought it would be wise to make those conclusions about him myself. I took a seat and had my notepad and pen ready to take notes. He welcomed us to his workshop and was expressing his excitement with the turnout. He went on to introduce his workshop series focused on literacy strategies for Saudi students. A fellow teacher shouted out, "What literacy?" Chuckles followed suit from several other colleagues.
The man chuckled and said, "Well, that's what we are here. These people are savages and have no concept or interest in reading. They are an oral-based society, so it is our job to teach them what's right."

I couldn't believe my ears. I surveyed the room, and people were nodding their heads in agreement with the statements this man just said. I was appalled by the ignorance and the colonialist mentality that many of these educators brought to the Kingdom. It made me sick to my stomach. I could feel my face turning red, and I felt hot and irritable. I quickly left the room as I could no longer tolerate the level of ignorance. I scurried to my office, and I just started to cry. How the hell can we progress and move forward as a society if these microaggressions and implicit biases persist?

After some alone time in my office and drinking a much-needed warm cup of tea, I decided it was best to approach my Chair and discuss what had happened in today's workshop. As I began to explain, she looked at me and said, "Thank you for sharing this with me; I will speak to the Dean about this matter." I had left the Chair's office, confident that he would be reprimanded for his actions.

I found out later, through the grapevine, that he got a little slap on the wrist, and they pretended it never happened. That was, unfortunately, the kind of thing that happened in the Kingdom. My experience taught me that people who rub shoulders or have friends in high places are untouchable. They have *wasta* –a term used in the Kingdom to indicate that a person has connections. And guess who feels the brunt of these actions? Our students! They know when teachers genuinely care about their well-being or that they are only there because they are offered a generous salary that their native countries could never provide them. Many teachers take these contracts with extrinsic motivations (money and prestige) and disregard intrinsic motivations to teach these students (passion, purpose).

Culture bashing is a significant phenomenon amongst the expatriate circles, and it's just utterly disgusting.

Lesson: You are in their land. Have the respect to learn about their customs and traditions. Don't judge a book by its cover.

The Cell Phone in the Classroom

———————◆●◆———————

State-of-the-art phone technology is in the hands of the youth. Saudi young college females are not an exception. They come to class with their cell phones only!

The old artifacts (notebooks, books) that, not too long ago, were used so wisely to take notes on each word our teachers explained in class, are no longer in existence.

My classroom was genuinely impersonal. The lesson delivery was influenced by internet searches conducted at that moment. Although technology allowed us to bring current information and data to be immediately merged in my lesson, it was also true that all-time critical theories of leadership were left out due to lack of time.

I lament that the photography of students was not allowed in Saudi classrooms. Imagine this scene: girls covered by their black *abayas* sitting with their immovable eyes and speedy fingers on the small cell screen! My Saudi students did take pictures of presentations, e-books, any resources used in class.

Not only the technology has changed the way we, professors, deliver our teaching, but it has transformed the way our students learn.

The critical thinkers of our past classrooms, those passionate theoretical fighters, are extinct. The new generations speak the internet language. Vocabulary is based on codes that rapidly summarize their thinking. But unbelievable things can also occur with the arrival of cell phones in the classroom: Tech-cheaters! I once caught a student masked by her abaya, who took a picture of the screen of her online test, emailed it to a classmate, who returned the correct answers in a text message. Pretty tech clever!

Lesson: Thinking about our own thinking, the metacognitive strategy for comprehension cannot be replaced by any technological device.

Using Mobile Phones to Overcome
Language Barriers in the Classroom

The university academic life was not always pleasant. There were parts of it that I disliked, such as reading and grading assignments and examinations.

Those assessment pieces made me aware of either the little effort students were putting into their education or the inappropriate teaching we as faculty, were still using in the classroom within confined walls.

There were many more things that I liked about academia that made me balance my dislikes and frustrations. One of those challenges during my academic exposure in Saudi was my English Language Learners, using technology to discover the world.

A few years ago, it did not cross my mind that I would spend time teaching ELL students whose background knowledge was conditioned to religion, family traditions, and government restrictions. The journey was fascinating but challenging.

Students were glued to their cell phones, smartphones, any device that had a camera attached. Their mobile phones were their lives, wants, needs, emotions, and food for their souls. In other words, students would not accept the possibility of being away from their mobile phones.

In the past, it could be considered an addiction; and I believe it should be treated as such. Teaching uninterested, emotionally disengaged, educationally unmotivated, knowledge apathetic, and passionately dispirited students were not fun. Many reasons could be attributed to the virtual face-to-face classroom phenomenon.

I attribute the first reason to a newly born university still battling with trials and errors academically and administratively. The institution was always redefining what it would like to be when it grew up. Will it be a teaching institution? A research organization? Or both? Depending on the decision the institution made, university life would dramatically change, and consequently, teaching would be approached differently in a more rigorous academic environment with clear policies and regulations.

Lesson: Best teaching practices in a classroom environment glued to faster responses given by a tech device are facing failures.

Assessment Changes are Not Allowed!

As a faculty, I was surprised to learn that my syllabus must contain X, Y, Z assessment practices, regardless of the curriculum content of the subject. That happened in the Kingdom.

The circumstances of your class content, the theoretical significance, and the performance progress become irrelevant if you cannot complete eight assessments during the semester. For each course, you should submit eight forms to evaluate the content — for example, midterm and final exams plus short quizzes, essays, projects, presentations, reports, demonstrations, technology use, among others. The importance of this story does not reside in the number of assessment practices to evaluate a class. Instead, it is about the number of students and the number of courses associated with the number of assessments required!

I was teaching a total of ten undergraduate courses. Each class had eight assessment strategies. One had a minimum of 30 students. After calculating all those numbers, 2400 assessments were submitted by 300 students to be graded before the final exam was completed. Today, I wonder why my mood was always disturbed, my unhappiness was my day-to-day mode of living, and my stress level was higher than ever.

As of today, I do not know how I survived the reading and grading of 2400 assessments without being insane or beating up someone. In retrospect, when I examine my life in Saudi, I did not have one. Although I wanted to balance my life, I could not.

Thinking about having a healthy eating strategy, a spiritual way of living and physical movements was a utopia. The time I spent reading papers, grading papers, and inputting grades in the

Blackboard system did not permit me to carry over personal and healthy professional modus of Operandi. I read all those papers written by girls who were not convinced about their future professional careers, papers written with disdain. Reflecting on their writings, I realized that I did not expand my content knowledge, but I did learn cultural modes. My primary learning allowed me to appreciate my home institution more, the three courses I taught, and the forty-five students I interacted with! I learned to appreciate my academic freedom more than ever.

I hope that I have made changes, created new ways of assessing, infused innovative strategies in the classroom, listened to learn and read to understand more. I truly regret that it did not happen while teaching in an undergraduate Saudi classroom. The curriculum and assessment imposition avoid faculty to be more into their love for what they do best: teaching.

Lesson: You do not appreciate what you have until you don't have it any longer.

State of the Art Technology

———————————◆●◆———————————

When we think about the Arab world, we make assumptions that sometimes can be confirmed, but other times can be misleading.

The state of technological advances in the Middle Eastern countries has surpassed what we assume these countries represent in our western-oriented perceptions. The technology advances in the Kingdom can be easily observed in the set-up of the classrooms. The curriculum discussions happening in departmental meetings have solidified the vigorously researched impact that technology has on the learning process of students.

With technology in the classroom, my colleagues said that their students gained control of their education, they could learn at their own pace, and they could access current events around the world that could make them rethink their ways of living in Saudi.

I found that state-of-the-art technology, when appropriately used, could enhance the learning experience and, many times, increase student performance. It is also true that excessive exposure to technology in the classroom, as well as the abusive use of cellular phones as a means to increase participation in the classroom, did have their limitations, beginning with students' social skills.

The vast use of technology created selfish individuals with poor social skills. The abusive use of technology affects our communication skills, making it difficult to interact openly and to integrate what they knew by connecting the new knowledge they added. I experienced isolation and confrontation in the classroom due to the misuse of the mobile phone to investigate content on the internet. The digital media literacy of my students shocked me many times. They could access, understand, participate, or create content using digital media. The use of cell phones to learn specific content demonstrated higher retention and academic productivity.

However, I also witnessed the social distances between the girls with enough money to upgrade their mobiles as soon as a new edition came out from those who were attending the university under scholarships granted due to lower socioeconomic backgrounds. Their access to technology advances was limited.

It was so obvious how technology was severely reinforcing social classes between them. Although I celebrated to have a classroom environment full of technological gadgets, I regretted not being able to approach my students more humanely.

Lesson: Not all that glitters is gold

Assessment Presentations Using Technology

At any higher education institution, class presentations are standard practices used by most professors.

There are different types of presentations. One example is a straightforward delivery of a chapter from the textbook to receive a cumulative score. Another type includes a group presentation in which contents of the course are delivered, examined, and analyzed by an individual or a group formed for that purpose. A combination of lecture, technology infusion, and interactive delivery would also be used by a group of students to make the teaching of the curriculum content more engaging and with a high comprehension level.

For any of these presentation variations, a rubric was used to determine the fidelity, integrity, and appropriateness of the content examined. The use of a rubric ensures that the student is aware of how she would be evaluated and the final grade that she would obtain if properly utilizing the metrics. However, Saudi female students decided not to use it. They did whatever they found was more comfortable with fewer complications and of course, less learning. I speculated on reasons for not using the rubrics.

Later I realized that although they are technologically well informed, they searched for presentations that were already on the internet and did not care about the alignment of the presentation to the rubric. Most presentations failed the rubric. Besides, of course, most presentations were of low quality, too wordy, with zero engagement level and with shallow consideration for the learning of their classmates.

At the end of the presentations, I raised questions, and I confirmed that they did not do what was expected of them. They did not frame others' learning according to the goals of the presentation. They also demonstrated that using technology to drive their curriculum presentations was a skill they did not possess. Their use of technology is limited to cell phone to access the internet, use of social media, and the utilization of a laptop as a typing machine.

Lesson: ***Curriculum drives the use of technology in the classroom, not the other way around.***

Social Life

For this book, social life in Saudi Arabia refers to an individual's interpersonal relationships with other people within their immediate surroundings.

The chapter on social life explores the different combinations of relationships that during our time living in Saudi, we formed with others.

The stories shared are about the close and intimate interactions that happened between Saudi and Non-Saudi males and females. There is a variety of social statuses of expatriates who come to live either temporarily or permanently in the Kingdom. In many circumstances, they identified themselves as single, divorced, married, with a significant other as a companion back home, with a fiancé, widower, or any other non-conventional type of relationship between two people.

Some of the stories we shared are based on some of our personal experiences. Other stories were mentioned to us during our time there by some of our colleagues. One story talks about the taste of the prohibited fruit, a male expatriate with a Saudi female, or stories of proposals and engagements by male Arabs to a female expatriate. Thankfully, the marriage proposals ended amicably. We examined the love affairs that we all knew existed, but that no one talked about.

The social life chapter includes stories of two expatriates who became intimately closer, but they both were very aware that dating was known as a temporary game. It also goes into the cultural codes and social protocols followed by both males and females, regardless of their social condition. Uniquely, Saudi females and males have become extraordinarily creative in terms of establishing the first contacts with people different from those arranged by their families. The use of mobile phones, for example, for secret dating, is prevalent among young adults.

In Saudi, the social restrictions of the family environment and the social regulations of the government made social life challenging to navigate. It encouraged individuals to spend excessive amounts of time with the same people doing the same activities regularly.

The consequences of the time spent together could evolve as pure friendship, partying, casual relationships, and even sexual intercourse.

The Forbidden Fruit

A single woman in Saudi Arabia can find herself in deep temptation.

I found myself trapped in the garden of Eden, continually being tempted to bite into the forbidden fruit.

I would casually walk through the mall, and I would see handsome, tall Saudi men wearing freshly pressed white *Thobes*, and their *Shemagh* styled in expressive ways.

They wore carefully, curated, freshly lined up beards, which meant they paid attention to detail, and cleanliness was important to them. They would walk with a commanding presence, and behind them, they would leave a trail of the majestic scents of the middle east, enticing foreigners to follow their trail—wanting more.

There were many occasions where my eyes would lock with handsome locals. For those three seconds, the world around us would stop, and the sound of our breath would heighten. I'd wonder how he would touch me. How would his lips feel pressed against mine? A quick dose of reality – it was not permitted to think this way, I thought. But those three seconds were some of the most pleasurable three seconds a single woman could have. The thought of being desired was like an aphrodisiac. It was all I needed.

Lesson: Imagination can be the most intensified form of foreplay.

An Expat Female Tasting the Prohibited Fruit

I heard about the stories of dating but could not imagine how complicated it was to date in Saudi Arabia when you are a female expatriate.

It is well known that a female expatriate can stir up quite the attention of a Saudi male. Western women are highly sought after by any other nationality in this region. The relationship between them was more permissive, transparent, and to the point. Saudi males are splendid, exquisite, and very complacent. Due to the hidden subculture that exists, a Saudi man knows exactly where to take his beloved foreigner on a date.

It is also known that there are clandestine apartments shared by more than one Arab male being used as secret hideouts where they bring their dates for a lovely evening rendezvous. These places prevent both parties from being questioned by the religious police—commonly known as the *mutawa*, in public sites.

In these obscure places, female expatriates spend long evenings and weekends with their secret lovers. Dating a Saudi male implies to do some homework about cultural miscues. First of all, age is a factor. The majority of Saudi males in their late 20s are married with children. Some of them reveal that fact as the polygamist condition of the culture, having a second wife is not perceived as a negative element in the relationship.

On the other hand, some may refrain from their marital condition. Usually, a Muslim male is acutely aware that a western woman does not deal well with the idea of getting involved with a married man. During the time spent together, the question of marriage is always present.

For a Saudi male, marriage is the normal consequence of dating. For a female expatriate, marriage is a commitment that implies more than a few months together. A female expat has different reasons to date a Saudi man. Having a love interest in Saudi Arabia as a female expat could be quite beneficial. You can get driven around and be showered with expensive gifts!

Lesson: Cultural differences must be overcome prior to enter into a serious relationship that could bring sentimental consequences forever.

Dr. Jeckle/Mrs. Hyde

There is an unfortunate truth that as an expat living in KSA, you make friends with people that you usually would not associate yourself within your native country. My friends and I called it "Living in the Saudi bubble." It meant that based on our circumstances, we would commit, allow, or accept certain things that we normally wouldn't.

I had the misfortune of becoming acquainted with a young woman who had left her life behind in London, England, in search of a new one. Ashamed of her Middle Eastern roots, she desperately wanted to be accepted as a white, female-identifying "Westerner" and was willing to go to extreme levels to do so.

For the sake of this story, I will call her Sarina. When I first met Sarina, I thought she was an elegant and well-refined British expat. She was charming, had a captivating allure to her, spoke with a sense of calmness and confidence. She arrived at the Kingdom a few weeks before I did, and already had things figured out!

When I met her, she had already found herself a boyfriend! She seemed to be extremely level-headed and focused on a larger goal. It was after getting to know her and spending most of my lunch breaks with her that she revealed her urgency in wanting to get married and have children.

I felt sorry that she was living with these parental and societal pressures, and I guess I slowly turned into a person she could confide in without judgment. Our lunch meetings turned into after school and evening dates, where we would sit and discuss her issues over homemade wine.

When she drank, the once 'full of light,' refined woman transformed into a dark, deceptive figure. All of her demons would unleash, and she would reveal many of her hidden truths. She would say that I needed to open my eyes and 'play the game.' "How many of these people are you going to stay in touch with when you leave?" Play the game; take what you can get from them." It got me thinking, is everyone playing this game? It turns out, Sarina wasn't the only one.

In the expat circle, plenty of people use each other for whatever connections they may provide. For example, many expat women make friends with men who drive so that they can save on hiring a driver. Some people make friends with the recommended winemaker on the compound so that they can put an end to their "jonesing" and get hookups on wine. Some people use their friends for their social networks and to gain access to exclusive events and five-star compounds. The Kingdom truly is a mirage.

Nothing was as it sometimes seemed, including friendships.

Lesson: Don't get desperate, associate with the people you would normally associate yourself with. The game always comes to an end.

A Saudi Love Affair

There's an adage that asserts, "One finds love when they least expect it."

My voyage to the Arabian Desert did not lead me to believe that I would find love there. I met Abdulaziz in a casual fashion. One evening, I finished work and headed home. I stopped in the management office to inquire about a parcel I was expecting to receive. There stood a tall, slender, handsome Saudi man. An impressionable man, to say the least. We exchanged glances for a quick moment and then off I went to my residence. That evening, Ravi—the housing manager—came to my villa and gave me a piece of paper with a phone number on it. "He liked you...he's expecting your call, Madam," I looked at Ravi with a confused look.

"Ok, thanks," I replied. I closed the door and glared down at the piece of paper. I kept thinking to myself, what does he want? Why is he interested in me? I didn't even look my best when our paths crossed.

That evening, I tried to distract myself from thinking about what had occurred a few hours prior. I kept pacing back and forth, thinking, should I call, or should I forget about? Was this a test? Is this some trap? I made the decision that I wouldn't do anything out of impulse and that if I still felt the desire to call him, then I would do so. The next morning, I called Abdulaziz. It was the beginning of our love affair.

Lesson: The heart wants what it wants.

Adventures with Abdulaziz

I looked forward to spending time with Abdulaziz. He was handsome, educated, well-rounded, and had a charismatic presence to him. He was also funny, charming, and spontaneous. He would pick up the phone and say, "Habibi, what are you doing this weekend?" Let's go to Bahrain and enjoy a much-needed getaway" or, "I'm on my way to pick you up for some shisha and BBQ along the Corniche." He turned many of those lonely nights into evenings filled with laughter and splendor. We would spend frequent time together, and we would discuss business ideas, politics, and our love for travel. It amazed me to hear his stories of when he studied at Stanford University. It made me realize that I had a preconceived notion of him. I stereotyped him as the privileged Saudi male that probably paid his way through school. He was quite the contrary. He was intelligent, ambitious, and tenacious—all of which was a recipe for success.

While we were both physically attracted to each other, our relationship flourished on an intellectual level. We inspired one another, and whenever we would see each other, we would know that it would be time well spent. This would go on for several months. I was starting to fall in love with a man that came from a completely different society than I did. He taught me how a man should treat a woman. He set a standard that I will be eternally grateful for. Sometimes we forget our worth, and in the strangest ways, we encounter lessons that teach us what we should and should not put up with. Our worlds came together, and although we tried to ignore it, the time came to address our feelings for one another.

Lesson: Open yourself up to the wonderful possibilities the world has to offer.

Abdulaziz' Proposal

———————◆●◆———————

My feelings towards Abdulaziz grew fonder each time I would spend with him. I made a conscious decision to keep him a secret because I did not want to draw any attention to my private life. No one knew about Abdulaziz. I liked it that way.

One evening, Abdulaziz decided to pick me up and take me out to the Movenpick hotel for a grilled seafood dinner, accompanied with shisha. It was our usual date night, and like other moments spent together, we would converse about everything from politics, religion, business, and love. In some respects, I felt like we were the Arab version of Marc Anthony and Cleopatra. I was feeling a complete high over discussions of global dominion. He casually took a draw from his shisha, and said, "I want to tell you something...something that I've meant to tell you for quite some time." He handed over the hookah, and I began to inhale the grape-mint flavored tobacco. "I want you to know that I have fallen in love with you, and I need to be honest with you about something very important." Not knowing what to expect, I exhaled my shisha smoke, and hesitantly replied, "Ok." "I am married." I was taken aback.
I felt a sudden pressure on my chest as if something had just ripped my heart right out.

"Excuse me?" I replied.

"I knew you would react this way, but it's not what you think. She knows about you."

"She knows about me?" It was like I couldn't even process the first blow, and now this? How does she know about me?

"I haven't kept you a secret. My wife knows about you, which is why I want to discuss something very important with you." Feeling an array of emotions, I let him proceed with what he had to say. "I have my wife's blessing, and I would like to ask you for your hand in marriage and having you as my second wife." Honestly, this was a first. How do you react to that when this is just something you're not accustomed to hearing? My natural reaction was to be sarcastic, and I asked, "What, your first one wasn't enough?"

He chuckled and said, "No, she's plenty, and she's a wonderful woman, but I had to marry her. It was arranged that way." He looked at me with a serious and affectionate look and expressed his love, admiration, and respect for me. He said, "Your first wife is the one you have to marry; your second wife is the one you want to marry." You are everything I could have ever wished and imagined, and I'm in love with you...truly in love with you." He began to tell me that he was well aware that this may not sit well with me or that this was something I was not accustomed to and to take all the time I needed to consider this proposal seriously.

The air was heavy, and it wasn't because of the shisha smoke.

Lesson: I knew that I could not love him fully if his heart did not entirely belong to me. Sometimes, you just have to let things go.

Dating as a Temporary Game

Dating in Saudi Arabia is a matter of high risk. While I was there, I identified three types of relationships: dating between expatriates, dating between a female expat with a Saudi male, and dating between a Saudi female with an expat male. This story is about dating between expatriates.

The relationship between expatriates usually grows due to the loneliness, isolation, and segregation that two foreigners of different gender face in this Muslim land. Dating, which is a natural human interpersonal behavior, can become a very dangerous situation. There are no places to go and meet without the fear of the presence of the religious police. Freedom and open dating are an upsetting situation.

A couple needs to be extremely careful to avoid any legal consequences. Also, before expatriates come to Saudi, they have their personal stories. Some are willing to share honestly or not to share and take the opportunity to date someone whose availability condition is identifiable. The risk of dating an expat is that he usually has left someone behind in his home country, who is waiting patiently for him or her. An affair between expatriates is something that becomes known, but no one talks about it. Many expatriates, particularly women, have received significant surprises when suddenly the wife of her expat boyfriend appears with the kids and the pet! The other surprise is when the male expat talks about an "ex-girlfriend" that never was such, but that was the tool used to capture and involve the female expat. Those two situations seem to be ruling the dating system between expatriates in Saudi, in which the restrictions to date are more severe than at any other country in the GCC region.

When dating in Saudi, the couple should clearly define in the first conversation what type of relationship they are willing to accept. Due to the isolation and solitude, two people can get involved in a loving relationship, not realizing that at any moment, one of them may be seriously hurt. Honesty is not what rules the relationship between two expats in Saudi. The forbidden, harsh, and oppressive environment usually determines the direction, complications, and consequences of the dating process.

A love affair in Saudi is also part of the job contract. When your contract ends, so does your love affair!

Lesson: Love and loneliness can lead to a dramaturgical scene of pain and regret.

Unpredictable but Required
Cultural Codes

Although the subordination of Arab women to men is typically enforced in their societies, it is also true that the extent varies by country.

Saudi females have more restrictive conditions than they do in Egypt and Lebanon, where they have hassle-free restrictions. These Muslim societies share similar cultural codes; among them, men standing when women enter a room. Unfortunately, as Westerners, lack of cultural codes and competencies when visiting Middle Eastern countries at-large, make us look insensitive, disrespectful, and inappropriate.

After my arrival at KSA, I met a few colleagues who lived in the same compound. They helped me acclimatize and adapt to the unknown social and cultural protocols. On Saturdays, we used to have dinner together outside the compound. There was a favorite Thai restaurant in downtown Khobar. At this place, I learned my first lesson of cultural regulations: "respect the different living areas for men and women." Yes, I learned that women do not eat or socialize in the same room as men. I also got my second lesson as they met some of their Arab female friends: "do not shake hands with an Arab woman unless she offers her hand first." Of course, I made the mistake that later was transformed into a cultural lesson. Almost every day I had a new lesson. I became mindful of not talking in public to an Arab man unless it was business-related (e.g., a question in the store to purchase something). Another lesson learned related to engaging in a conversation with an Arab male unless we have been formally introduced. Even more, do not maintain eye contact and talk in private.

When introduced to another woman, a Latina tends to use very unconventional cultural rules. For example, we ask questions about what she does, where she comes from, whether or not she has other siblings, if she is single or married, among other inquiries. Although it is true that Latin American culture share similar cultural codes with Arabs, the previous questions are normally asked between two women but not between a woman and a man. In the Latino culture, we do not express surprise as we talk about the number of siblings in a family. We joke about how fertile our parents were! We connect large families with the lack of technology, television sets, and or any other type of entertainment in the old times. There is an indirect way of saying that our parents enjoy sex, and children were a sign of virility. I learned that in Saudi, large families give the father the prestige of virility as well.

On my hours of solitude, I thought about the concept of family as a social unit. Family loyalty and obligations are first, then friends and jobs. I found many similarities with Arab culture. We keep the elderly with us; the concept of nursing homes and assisted living centers are non-existent in both Arab and Hispanic communities. A child is expected to care for his/her parents in their advanced age.

In my cultural analogy, the idea of a son as a provider of honor, whereas a daughter as a source of shame, was pervasive in both cultures. In both cultures, faith means the futuristic representation of God's willingness to make things happen. We both believe that most things are controlled by the will of God (fate). *'In shā' Allāh* is the Arabic language expression for "*God willing*" or "*if God wills.*" In Spanish, we use the word "*Ojala y Dios quiera*" to claim the happening of future events thanks to God, without the intervention of human beings.

Soon, I started feeling closer to the culture for our similarities and not our differences.

I reflected on the historical context of the domination of the south of Spain by Arabs for more than 800 years and that Spaniards blended and later spread their genetic and Arab cultural mannerisms to the Americas when transformed into "conquistadores" imposed their language, their religion, their social behaviors and protocols to all of us, Latinos.

Lesson: You don't realize how similar cultures can be until you face your own cultural competencies with the ones that dominate the culture you are adopting temporarily.

Cell Phone for Secret Dating

Cellular phones are the most used technological artifact for communication on the planet. Regardless of socioeconomic status, most people have a cell phone, have used one, or have known about the existence of that type of phone.

In Saudi, the use of mobile phones has augmented dramatically over the past decade. Mobile phones are now a vital part of social life. Cell phone technology is changing the way young females meet and date in the Kingdom of Saudi Arabia.

The young population, with a luxurious lifestyle, adopt the most updated version of digital interaction not only for communication purposes but also for reinforcing their social images, an essential aspect of who they are. They are very savvy in the use of mobile phones to the degree that exclusive models and numbers are created for their personal use. It is normal to see a young Saudi with more than two cell phones. In my classroom, the students revealed that they have an additional telephone only for dating. They explained that texting and, more recently, Bluetooth technology is breaking down barriers.

They agree that the majority of women have found discreet ways around romance in the most conservative, oppressive, and religiously strict society in the world. Young Saudi females go to malls, shopping centers, among other places, and connect with young males through Bluetooth. Their names appear on the cell, and from there, a later phone call will set the initial encounter. One of the many consequences of the mobile phone is that it may break, in the near future, the "matching process" traditionally used by Muslim parents to pair their daughter to a man they pre-selected to marry her. The impact of the cell phone may change that cultural custom sooner than later.

Lesson: He/she who made the rules also created ways to deceive them.

The Saudi Bachelor Pad

I met Qasim on my compound. He worked as a national guard, and every time he would see me, he would smile and lower his gaze. One day, as I was coming home from grocery shopping, he saw that I was struggling with my bags and helped carry them into my villa. "You are very beautiful," he quietly muttered under his breath.

"Thank you," I replied.

I asked him for his name, and he replied, "Qasim." He smiled, left my villa, and resumed his post, guarding the compound with a new sense of pride.

One afternoon, I finished my regular teaching shift and returned home. In front of my villa, I found a gift bag with three small bottles of Oud and a note that read, "Please meet me tonight outside the compound, Qasim." As I opened the bottles, sniffing them one by one, I quickly became aroused. My imagination ran wild, and I instantly fantasized about kissing Qasim. That evening, I got myself ready and put on my favorite scent of the three, grabbed my *Abaya*, and wrapped myself with it. I took my headscarf and wrapped it over my head twice, like a real Saudi. I put on my *niqab*—which wasn't mandatory, but I used it to keep my identity a secret. There was some power in that. I grabbed my purse and left my villa. As I walked towards the gates, I kept thinking, "What if this guy rapes me or kills me? I'm all alone…" For some reason, my instincts lead me to believe otherwise. Qasim didn't give off the rapist vibe. As I exited the compound, I walked a block, and there was his car, idling as he waited for me. I walked towards the car, and he lowered the passenger window and smiled at me. "*Yalla*," he exclaimed. I quickly got in, and we drove off, leaving the compound behind. I suddenly got a feeling of rush and excitement. He's playing Rabeh

Saqer, and his car smelled like an elixir of sandalwood and musk. He lit a cigarette and offered me a drag.

"I don't smoke cigarettes," I exclaimed.

"No? Do you like shisha?" he asked.

"Yes, sometimes I smoke shisha," I replied.

"Khalas, then you smoke cigarettes," and he began to laugh. His smile was contagious: Beautiful dimples, lovely teeth, and the shadow that swiped across his face that made him look so sexy.

"Where are we going?" I asked.

"I am taking you to a special place. You'll like it," he responded.

After driving for nearly thirty minutes, we arrived at an apartment building. He gave me a set of keys and told me to exit the car, enter the building and go to the 4th floor, apartment 411. He assured me that he would meet me in the apartment in a few minutes. I can't lie, I was beginning to freak out, thinking that I had been set up or something terrible was going to happen. I asked him, why couldn't we go in together? He replied, "Because there might be the religious police, and we will get in trouble." That made sense, I thought. I quickly made my way into the apartment lobby and took the stairs four floors up. I surveyed the numbers and found the apartment. I inserted the key, turned the lock, and opened the door. It was beautiful. There were candles everywhere and rose petals across the floor. It was so intimate.

As I walked into the apartment, I saw that there was a projector, big screen tv, entertainment system, video games, shishas –you name it. I went into the kitchen, and I opened the fridge to find it filled with soft drinks and alcohol. I opened the cupboards and found no dish sets or cutlery. There were just plastic bags with extra charcoal for the shisha, paper cups, and lighters. After my investigation, I sat on the sofa and waited for Qasim to enter. I was beyond confused. Was this his place of residence? I had all these questions brewing in my mind to ask him. Qasim came to the apartment with a bag filled with snacks and more soft drinks. "Do you like it?" he asked.

"It's nice...is this your house?" I replied.

"No, this is an apartment; my friends and I share. It's our place to escape." It was their version of a clubhouse or a man cave. A space that they could make their own and do whatever they pleased...away from their parents. I discovered that Qasim spent several hours a week at this bachelor pad. It was an escape for him to indulge in his vices (shisha, video games, and women). He grabbed my hand and told me how he had fantasized being alone with me and kissed me. I told him that if he was looking for sex, he was looking in the wrong direction. He laughed and said, "No sex tonight; just your company is fine." We smoked shisha, ordered in, and watched a movie that evening. It was a nice getaway from compound life.

Lesson: Sometimes you have to shake things up to gain insight into an underground world.

Empowerment

In the Kingdom landscape, the definition of empowerment would be taken as a cynical term since it refers to the empowerment of a woman.

In this book, we used the operational definition of empowerment to denote the process that occurs in the classroom to Saudi females as they realized how strong they were, the level of confidence they had, the ability to control their own lives by claiming their rights, softly.

The term empowerment may have different meanings to different people. The personal experiences, the circumstances where empowerment takes place, the hopes created by being empowered, and the right to dream as being enabled are all elements of empowerment.

In this chapter, empowerment was examined from the perspectives of the lessons that students and teachers shared to move forward. It also involved the educational reforms taking place in the Kingdom that have positively influenced females in particular. Other issues, such as women's leadership and entrepreneurship (legal or illegal), were carefully appraised through real stories of real people.

Women empowerment through education is part of the new educational policies overtaken in Saudi classrooms. The policies are an invitation for curriculum changes and modifications. Among the many innovative policies in Vision 2030, the reform report is the removal of the responsibility of education from the tutelage of the religious establishment. In this section, we talk about the state-of-the-art technology of higher education and the elaborate use of social media that is enforcing changes in the faculty teaching delivery modes.

Women's leadership deserves special treatment in this chapter. The stories gathered around the transformation from girl to woman, due to many circumstances and the misperception on the definition of leadership for boys, not for girls. We also included the dress code as a positive effect on the empowerment of women. Saudi females as they travel have the choice of not wearing the traditional attire, *abaya*. We learned that women feel the empowerment and liberation of a deprived dress code back home.

Wine making, no way!!!

Human beings find their ways to overcome deprivation and limitations. Alcohol consumption is prohibited everywhere in the KSA.

For example, medicines or prescription drugs that contain a minimum amount of alcohol are not only banned but also replaced by other remedies. Even the mouthwash that has a regulated dose of alcohol cannot be sold in the stores.

Before going to KSA, I read about alcohol drinking and its severe restrictions. However, short enough after my arrival, I learned that there are other ways to defy, violate, and disrupt those rules: by making craft wine.

Believe it or not, there are winemakers in the Kingdom! Some with experience in the field of winemaking, and some others very novice in the art of wine production. The difference is noted because some could be excessively sweet or sour. In general, the small output forces the winemaker to transform the closet of the house into the winery room. Sometimes it is only for friends who are willing to cooperate by not telling anyone about the winemaking. They also agree to purchase a bottle for an extremely high amount of money, regardless of the quality of the product.

Living in the Kingdom, I realized that I was willing to pay any amount of money for something I could not find. The wine was one of those items.

In talking to friends, other expatriates, they confessed that they had gone the extra mile to get a bottle of wine at least once or twice a year. However, they were not willing to risk themselves again by attempting to acquire camouflaged wine from someone who knew someone who made wine!

I bought a bottle of red wine from a Chilean winemaker. I hid the bottle under my *abaya* and brought it to my compound. The taxi driver did not know that he just helped me commit a crime. I used only a few drops of the wine, as it was too expensive to share with anyone! I sometimes used it for cooking and waited for a special holiday to drink a quarter of the glass.

Based on our observation, when a person is denied access and is restricted to something, it creates an intense desire and craving. We believe that the winemakers in the Kingdom have no idea on how expatriates coming from wine-drinking countries genuinely appreciate the efforts they make. But the opposite is also true. As expatriates, we are very much aware that we refuse to accept that we are acting criminals and that we have become delinquents in the eyes of the Sharia law ruling the Saudi society. We were lucky!

Lesson: it is not about drinking; it is about being prohibited to drink.

Bootlegging in a Dry State

In KSA, it is forbidden to drink, distribute, or make alcohol. Individuals who suffer from alcoholism choose KSA as a destination to live and work to support their choice of 'drying out.' Unfortunately, this usually tends to backfire, and the restriction of alcohol only entices expats and locals to find creative ways to obtain it.

I was first introduced to alcohol in KSA at an expat party in a neighboring compound. I remember being offered a red party cup and was told not to ask, just drink. I remember hesitating to take a sip, thinking that it could have been cyanide and that my night would have ended right then and there.

As I looked around, I saw that everyone was drinking this concoction, so I figured...what the heck, why not? I drank what seemed to be wine. "How did they get wine in here?" I thought. I asked my friend how they were able to bring in contraband, and her response was, "It's homemade." I couldn't believe it. People were making moonshine, wine, and crafting their beers and ciders in the Kingdom. I felt like I was living in Al Capone's prohibition era. I was drinking something that I knew could potentially put me behind bars for a very long time or worse, killed. Alcohol was a substance that was forbidden. I can't even lie; it was exciting, and I was intrigued. I wanted to know more.

As I continued to sip the wine, I kept thinking about what I would add to this mysterious wine recipe to make it taste better. "What if I added oak wood chips to give it a smokier finish," I thought.

A girlfriend of mine who worked with me built a reputation for being the best wine supplier on the compound. I asked her to teach me the recipe for what was called "The red sea mixture." With her guidance, I made my first batch and added the oak wood chips as an experiment. Twelve weeks later, I called over a few girlfriends for a wine tasting. One of my friends gladly took the first sip, looked at me, and said, "You've hit gold here. This tastes like real wine." That moment marked the beginning of my clientele. Supply and demand, I officially became a bootlegger.

Lesson: Saudi Arabia isn't a place of confinement. It's a place filled with opportunity. You go there with one skill and you come out with ten.

I Left as a Girl and Returned as a Woman

When I decided to move to the Kingdom, I knew that I would return as a different person. I left as a young girl filled with insecurities, vulnerabilities, and lots of doubt. One might say, "Picking up and moving to Saudi Arabia takes a lot of courage." I couldn't agree more. It does take a lot of courage to leave everything you know, all of your comforts behind and start a new life in a new country, located halfway across the world. It was that kind of excitement, that zest for life and adventure that I desperately yearned for.

Saudi Arabia was my way out. It was my way to get out of my comfort zone, to take risks and believe in myself. A country criticized for its restrictive nature became my refuge. It was my desert rose. It taught me to find beauty where no one could. It taught me to look inwards and that if I wanted to improve on my self-worth, I had to do the work. I had all the time in the world to get to know me. I had never really enjoyed being alone or even saw the purpose of it. Saudi Arabia taught me to fall in love with myself, how to enjoy my own company, and appreciate everything that I had. I started dating myself and realized that that was the relationship I needed to truly work on. Two beautiful years of growing my mindset, hustling to make my dreams come true, learning about the power of saying 'No", and finding happiness in the little things contributed to the woman I am today. What began as a journey of risk-taking and vulnerability turned into an adventure of a lifetime.

Living in Saudi Arabia is one of my proudest accomplishments, and the experience wouldn't have been as productive and fulfilling if it were not for all of the people, mentors, and friends I encountered along the way. I thank them for reminding me of my strength and power.

I left Saudi Arabia with a full heart, ready to take on the world and chase after my wildest dreams. I am forever grateful.

Lesson: Be the change you wish to see in the world. You are enough.

Leadership is For Boys, Not Girls

While I was teaching a class titled Leadership & Teamwork to freshman females in Saudi, I felt excited about the unique opportunity to develop and nurture leadership behaviors, skills, and styles in my students.

Using my leadership training and knowledge about the socio-cultural restrictions, I convinced myself that I could make changes and transform my female students into effective leaders.

I dreamt about creating a classroom laboratory for leadership development. I visualized examples of leadership dilemmas. I fantasized that they knew how to harness the power inherent in the difficulties and mobilized people toward attaining goals.

Determined to cultivate female leaders, I crafted situations for the students. The focus was on developing trust, generating commitment, getting work done while building future performance capacity, integrating action and reflection, delegating, coordinating, resolving conflicts, and creating a shared vision while leveraging diversity. I accomplished all those skills and activities through different mechanisms of instruction and classroom engagement.

Towards the end of the academic semester, I asked them to demonstrate specific leadership actions to transform the community or the organization that they would lead or would like to lead.

Surprisingly, I experienced an image of paralysis in the classroom, until someone clearly said, "Leadership is for boys, not for girls."

I did not know what to do. I wanted to cry, thinking that I had wasted my time and my passion for the subject. I tried to help them realize the dormant leaders they had inside, their leadership skills, and the behaviors of those actions they perform daily.

I replied and asked why they see leadership as a male attribute and not a female strength. Some of the students stated that they do not need to lead because leadership was their father's role, not only in the family as the provider but also at work where they led hundreds of people.

I requested examples in which a father expressed his leadership behaviors and actions to benefit all their family members. Almost all wanted to participate by raising their hands and shaking their bodies. "My father selects my husband; he knows what is best for me." Another said, "My dad has a business, and he will put me in any position as soon as I graduate because he trusts that I am his daughter and that I will take grow our businesses. That's leadership. I do not need to be a leader". Another female argued that leadership skills are developed in boys genetically because they are stronger in the Arabic families. She reinforced that her brothers and her dad were the leaders in her family. She stated that they made all the decisions for her, her sisters, and her mom.

After that discussion, I reflected on the female leadership theories and models, realizing that there is no best way to lead and that leadership is cultural related.

Undoubtedly, women leadership has a different face in KSA.

Lesson: The desires of becoming a leader can be nurtured by the nature of the decision making you encourage in others.

The Empowerment of the Dress Code

The female students were all veiled before entering my classroom. Then suddenly, I saw them take off their *abayas*, and they seemed to fly with a sense of freedom! It may have been my perception. Perhaps I saw them with my Western-oriented mind.

It was the month of May, the end of the semester, during one of my leadership lessons related to women and leadership roles. The lesson started with the concept of empowerment. I asked if, in the Arab language, there was such a word. Some vocabulary words are non-existent in some languages — for example, the word resilience, does not exist in the Spanish language.

My students did not come up with a word that may have a different meaning or no meaning in the Arab language. For the class, we dismembered the compound word and defined its parts. "The root is power," they said. I started the interaction by asking, "Who gives you the power, and how do you use that power?"

Interestingly enough, one girl said, "Hiding behind my *abaya* gives me power." I did not expect that response.

According to Islam, women are expected to wear veils. Nevertheless, some countries in the region do not impose it upon them. Some of those countries are, for example, Egypt, Lebanon, and Syria. Although they may live the rigidity of their religious precepts and a strong sense of spirituality in their Islam practices, some women may choose not to wear veils in those countries. In Saudi, it is different.

Saudi women adhere to a more traditional dress code of wearing *abaya*, *jilbob*, or *chador*. Their *hijab* (veil) is mandatory by religious rules. However, regardless of when and where they wear their traditional dresses, these women empower themselves using non-traditional practices of empowerment.

Among them, they talk about their future, their desires, their needs, and wants. They speak with optimism as if they were in control of their lives. Soon, I realized that I was actively involved in a reflective conversation in which their empowerment rituals and manners were unrevealed. As they continued exploring how important it was to wear their traditional dress code, they also expressed that not wearing veils created fear and distress of mistreatment by fanatics or those that pretended to be guardians of Islam in Saudi society. At the same time, the dress code allowed them to rebel against a belief that concern for modesty was the main reason for the traditional dress code.

There is nothing modest under the veil, they said.

Their choices of outfits were far from simplicity and decorum. Under the veil, they felt empowered by the European and American attires they show off. I pushed the empowerment exchange further and raised questions on the impact of the dress code as they visited other countries.

Some said, "Dr. Ana, when you travel out of the country (KSA) next time, pay attention to Saudi women's movements before landing in another country."

Curiously, the next time I traveled from Damman airport, I did. As the flight was getting closer to our foreign land destination, before my eyes, the veiled women became unveiled creatures! Suddenly, they came out of the bathrooms carrying designers' outfits, beautiful make-up, and an outgoing, extrovert, and demonstrative attitude incomparable to the submissive mode adopted as they came into the airplane. Their *abayas* and *hijabs* stayed behind. They seemed to belong to another world, the one they left behind the veil!

As we continued the in-class analysis of women empowerment and traditional dress code, they talked about their concerns about traveling after 9/11. They referred to the relationship between dress code and discrimination, abuse, and mistreatment by people of the non-Muslim countries. They confirmed that the unforgettable 9/11 tragedy marked their lives with additional social complications when they go to places wearing their traditional dresses. They told stories of most devoted women refusing to uncover their faces as well as their bodies from veils and robes. These women have been the target of physical abuse by border customs, police and or any individual on the streets of the city they are visiting.

Lesson: The wings of my freedom are culturally attached to my dress code.

Entrepreneurship in the ESL Classroom

I loved challenging my students in the ESL classroom, and I was infamous for teaching outside of the box. I felt that while it was essential to adhere to a structured curriculum, language acquisition can be enhanced when students are allowed to express themselves creatively.

Instead of the traditional "choose a country and present it" final project, I challenged my beginner level ESL students to go above and beyond their newly acquired lexicon and combine their passion for entrepreneurship with English. I placed them in groups and told them that they were going to create businesses, and their ideas would be showcased in the student center. The students were tasked to come up with original business ideas, create a proposal, and present/mock sell their products.

When they came to class, they were inspired and ready to share their innovative ideas! Some of my colleagues thought that I was overly ambitious, assigning such a grand task to a beginner level ESL class. Right, I did push them. However, I believed in these girls. I felt like I would have been doing an injustice to these them, stifling their creativity and their imagination for the sake of repetitive grammar lessons. It was a risk I was willing to take, and I was beyond excited to see what these girls would create.

On presentation day, the groups huddled and worked together, setting up their respective booths. The level of attention to detail that these girls displayed was unbelievable. They created a complete marketing package including; signs with their logos, business cards, pamphlets, and one group even created their app! The level of pride and sophistication in their projects was extraordinary. Once the "marketplace" opened for business, students from all programs flocked to see what was going on.

With pride, these young entrepreneurs were conversing in English to their Saudi female counterparts about their businesses and their products. They discussed their inspirations and shared how empowered they were to have the opportunity to display their ideas amongst their peers. I recall one group creating an online music distribution service—like Spotify—for up and coming *Khaleeji* (Gulf) artists.

The passion and conviction that these girls displayed in their projects were remarkable and unforgettable. The chair of the ESL program came to congratulate me on the success of the marketplace project and was astonished to learn that these were beginner level students! I told her that the students found inspiration in their projects, and I ultimately found inspiration in them.

Lesson: Encourage creativity in your classroom. Let it be a space where dreams are nurtured, not suppressed.

Spirituality

The definition of spirituality in the Arab context is affiliated with religion — specifically, Islamism. The doctrine of Islam demonstrates peace and tolerance. As we connect spirituality and Islam, both involve a relationship with God. A spiritual person in general terms is someone whose primary aim is to love himself and others.

In the Arab world, the *Quran*, the sacred book, rules the practice of Islamism. The *Quran* possesses 114 units of varying lengths, known as *suras*. The sacred book involves all aspects of human existence. The *suras* are related not only to spirituality and ritual prayer but also to doctrine, social organization, and legislation.

The chapter on spirituality focuses on one of the authors' experiences in Mecca and Medina. The holiest city for Muslims, Mecca (Makkah, Arabic word), is the place where the Prophet Muhammad was born. For Muslims, at some point in their lives, they will visit Mecca. The city of Medina, on the other side, is historically known as the place where Prophet Mohammed began his campaign to establish Islam. Visiting both sites represent the maximum desire a Muslim person has before he or she dies.

We share stories of our spirituality and our mechanisms of practicing our religions in a country in which there is no freedom of religion. We, the expatriates, learned about private prayer gatherings and quickly assumed our limitations imposed by the ruling system in which Islamism is the official and only religion that can be publicly practiced.

We share stories about the social interpretation of the *Quran* and the role that a woman plays in Islam.

The personal narratives were constructed with broad experiences in the culture, as an example, the prayer time closure. Although the role of women in religion is considered a "heavy subject," the Saudi female friends and colleagues were open to talking about their views, practices, spirituality, and dancing to avoid becoming too serious on a topic that for them, is their soul and spirit. Without talking or arguing, it can be perceived that Saudi women will not change their spiritual practices because they are their way of life.

Mecca & Medina

One of the reasons I came to Saudi Arabia was partially due to my spiritual quest. When I was a child, I lived near a mosque, and the calls to prayer were hypnotic. The prayer right before the sun was setting was my favorite. I learned that this prayer was called *Maghrib.*

The hints of lavender, pinks, and oranges that spread across the sky were unbelievably magical, and the soothing sounds of the *athan* led me to believe that something beyond us was responsible for displaying such beauty before our eyes each evening.

When I think about twilight, a sense of nostalgia comes over me, steering me to that particular time in my life. Before my voyage to Saudi Arabia, I had embarked on a spiritual journey that led me to Islam. When asked about my search for Islam, I always used to say that Islam found me.

During my undergraduate years, I experienced a dream that was life-changing for me, at least, and partially responsible for my curiosity in Saudi Arabia. I dreamt that it was the end of times, and I was surrounded by all of society's ill doings and ill doers. I remember feeling my knees buckle and I suddenly collapsed to the ground, pleading that I always believed, I didn't know which religion to adhere to. To my right was a man in Islamic attire in *sajdah*—a prayer position, and he looked over to me and said, "As long as you believe." He commenced praying, and I suddenly woke up from the dream. I was completely drenched, and my heart was pounding out of my chest. That dream led me to the pursuit of understanding the concept of a higher being.

Throughout my university years, I became interested in learning more about Islam, and I took electives that explored pre-Islamic

Arabia and the inception of Islam into the region. I was fascinated and left the courses wanting more. I wanted to learn more about the religion, the culture, and the Arabic language. When the opportunity to teach in Saudi Arabia was presented to me, I made the conscious decision to visit Mecca and Medina. I truly believed that this teaching position came into fruition because the path was being constructed for me to make my pilgrimage to the Holy land. It was a promise that I knew I could not break. Somehow, someway, I had to make it to Mecca.

In June 2016, during the Holy month of Ramadan, I visited the Prophet's mosque in Medina and made my way to enter the Holy city of Mecca to do Umrah. I remember staring at the famous clock tower and couldn't believe that I was in Mecca. It is a dream for Muslims across the globe to experience Mecca, and it is one of the five pillars of Islam for a Muslim to complete in their lifetime. I kept thinking, "My God, how blessed I am to be here and experience this." I went with two converts- A British and an American, and we were truly astonished to see the Grand mosque.

We took off our shoes and carried them in bags and walked into the magnificent mosque. There were millions of people walking through a tunnel with green lights to reach the Kaaba. The mosque had so many levels, and people were circling the Kaaba and the multiple levels of the mosque. It looked like a black and white wave moving in a gentle circular motion. I looked at the Kaaba, and I just broke down in tears. I was in complete shock because I couldn't believe that I made it to Mecca. I saw men and women praying, people of all different cultural and ethnic backgrounds, unified under the same spirit and adoration for God. I remember thinking, "Why couldn't the outside world be more like Mecca?" Free from every "ism" you could think of.

I couldn't help but think of Malcolm X. When he visited Mecca, he expressed the same sentiments and argued that the West had a lot of 'growing up' to do when it comes to love and acceptance of all people, from all walks of life. Interestingly, when King Abdul-Aziz died, he was buried in an unmarked grave, and his body was wrapped in a simple white cloth. He did not leave this world with all of the riches he had acquired in this life. He left the way he came into this world; pure.

Mecca displays a spirit that can leave anyone grounded and speechless. It is a place where humility, compassion, and love are practiced.

Lesson: Mecca is truly where the world meets.

The Religious Practices of An Expatriate

At school, one of my colleagues asked me about the religion that I profess. I said without hesitation, "I was raised Catholic."

She replied, "Me too."

My colleague is from Nigeria, and she traveled to live in Khobar due to her husband's profession, a petroleum engineer who was hired by the Khobar Oil Corporation, the largest petroleum company in the world.

They both lived in the company compound, a very privileged place to live without abiding by the external KSA residents' rules and regulations. At the large oil compound of more than 30,000 inhabitants, petroleum workers from everywhere in the world, different religions were practiced. A Catholic priest would come from one of the vicinities' towns and provided service on Friday mornings at the elementary school gymnasium.

Nowhere else in Khobar or Damman or any other place in the Kingdom, would you find another type of religious service other than Islam precepts. One may think that Christians were able to participate in the services freely, but the reality was the opposite.

To profess my faith and execute my religious practices, I needed to have a friend living in the Khobar compound extend me an invitation. It did require approval from the CEOs of the company. A copy of my passport was required, the completion of some background forms, and I had to wait at least four weeks before being approved to visit the oil compound to attend the Christian mass.

Once I obtained my permit, I was able to not only attend the Catholic mass service but also to visit friends who I accidentally met after "church." My Nigerian colleague insisted on processing the "visitor permit" for me because she had heard my South American accent, and she wanted me to be able to interact with my counterparts from that side of the world.

The second time that I went to mass, I met two Venezuelans that I later became friends with. The times I attended the Saturday service, I noticed the presence of many buses with Filipino expatriates. I asked how they were allowed to come in large numbers to the exclusive ARAMCO compound. I was told that one of the agreements reached between the countries about the Filipino labor force was the freedom to profess their religious practices. The Saudi government made sure to comply with the accord.

I always wondered about the practice of our faith while being in Saudi. Was it because you are genuinely a faithful practitioner, or was it because there was no other thing to do? It may be both. In Saudi, entertainment is forbidden. There are no cinemas, dancing clubs, concerts, theatrical plays, etc. Foreigners are subject to adaptations for survival. Practicing your religion is a matter of surviving the challenging environment in which you live. I have to admit that the positive side of going to church contributed to enhancing my appreciation for my family traditions, values, and beliefs. By praying to God, I became more connected with my mother, my siblings, and my children.

Lesson: Religion becomes a tool for surviving difficult environments and leads to increase your own connection with your loved ones.

Prayer Time Closure

During my time in the Kingdom, there was a mandatory rule that enforced the closure of shops during prayer times. To put this into perspective, it is worth noting that in Islam, a Muslim is required to pray five times a day. The prayers are *al-fajr* (dawn prayer), *Zhuhr* (early-afternoon prayer), *Asr* (late afternoon prayer), *Maghrib* (sunset prayer) and *Isha* (night prayer).

A retail business would open at around 10 am, so this would mean that locals and expats would have four prayer calls to schedule their day around. To be productive, errands were to be done before the calls to prayer. If you were in a shop during prayer time, you would either be asked to leave the store and come back after prayer time. In the case of grocery shopping, you would be stuck in the store, going up and down the aisles for an additional half-hour until the cashiers resumed their posts. Prayer time was known as break time. The reality was that not everyone was praying. There were devout Muslims who would find the nearest prayer room to pray in the malls, but many used this time to go for a smoke break, make calls, or conduct personal matters.

Many expats would grow impatient of these prayer time closures as they knew that store merchants weren't going off to pray. I am aware that the Kingdom is going through quite the transformation, and this may be a dated protocol, but it's worth mentioning should you ever consider living and work in KSA.

Lesson: Plan strategically and structure your day around prayer times.

The Religion of Belly Dancing

Religion affiliation is essential to everyone in Arab society, especially women.

Most Arabs believe that the role of the woman is described in the *Quran*, the Islamic holy book. There is no question that the Kingdom has the privilege of having Mecca on its land. It makes the country unique and different from the rest of the Arab world. Male and female profess their Islamic faith at the same level, five praying times that include the first prayer at 4.00 am before the sunrises and the last prayer as the sun goes down. Although women do not share the main floor of the mosques, they observe the ritual of the Islam religion from a different angle of the Mosque than males. According to Islam, piousness, devotion is the most commendable feature that a Muslim woman can have.

On a Friday evening, I invited a group of women to my home. They were Muslims born in either in Saudi or born in other Arab countries, and expatriates from different religious faiths. The purpose of the gathering was tea, dates, and chocolates to talk about us, family, life. Suddenly, the conversation twisted on the role of the woman in the *Quran*. It ignited sentiments and strong positions on what the Muslim man interprets what that role is. They agreed on the fact that they are not directly mentioned in the holy book, but their presence is suggested.

In that exchange of ideas, we all learned about the diverse interpretations offered by men on the protagonist's function of females in the Quran. Based on that conversation, we concluded the role of the women in the holy book depended on the level of family control and request for obedience a male has from the women in his life. His role was unquestionably clear; however, that was not the fact for the Muslim woman. The discussion ended abruptly when the sound of Arabic music interfered in the heated give-and-take. Some jumped from the seats and started moving their bodies and bellies as we, the Western expatriates, dropped our jaws, seeing the sensuality of the figure movements that made us forget about the intensity of the unknown role of the woman in the Muslim world and religion.

Lesson: Dancing makes us forget the complexities of life circumstances.

Recommendations
if Visiting
Saudi Arabia...

For *Educational Reasons*:

1. Read the contract very carefully. Small and large prints have different meanings. Verify the dates of initiation and end of your contract.

2. Learn about the consequences of breaking the academic contract.

3. Negotiate your teaching contract. If you do not negotiate, you will learn that there are people who are doing the same work, and they are monetarily making more than you are.

4. Make a copy of your contract, highlight what you do not understand, and ask for clarifications before signing it.

5. Ask questions on class size, teaching workload, time for research, and professional development for your career enrichment.

6. Request the inclusion of a section of specifics about your research time, access, and delivery of your investigations not only locally but also internationally.

7. Solicit written responses from your supervisors on what type of research topics faculty and students could investigate in the classrooms.

8. Pose questions on the number of institutional, college, and or departmental committees you are expected to serve.

9. Look for an explanation of the different academic ranks and what entails to be in one of them. Before arrival in the Kingdom, ask what your academic responsibilities are in the educational status offered on your contract.

10. Clear misinterpretations on the number of credit hours per course as compared to the ones you know in your country of origin. Do not make any assumptions. They will not be interpreted the same at any university in the KSA.

11. Revise academic freedom practices at that specific institution. At the interview, ask for the level of independence in making curriculum changes on your syllabus, the freedom of changing assessment practices, the acceptable teaching methodologies, and technology demands, among other academic questions.

12. Demand clarifications in your contract on paid and unpaid leave of absences. Seek responses for leaving the country temporarily for important family affairs such as the graduation of a son/daughter, weddings of your children, funeral and memorials of your loved ones, close family illness. Verify the length of time of your paid leave.

13. Ask if the institution provides funding for research, conferences, and professional development workshops for their faculty members.

14. Request a list of reputable agents to obtain services for your Work visa. The government website provides a list of those agencies.

For *Social-Cultural Reasons*:

1. Learn about the social and acceptable protocols on the relationships between females and males, expatriates and non-expatriates, and any combination of the close interactions that may happen between expatriates and Arabs.

2. Understand your role as an expatriate. Be aware of what you can or cannot do in the country.

3. Learn on the use of cellular phones for different purposes, especially the dating patterns that originated by using it.

4. Study the environment of food as a relationship with others. Before accepting an invitation to eat, make sure that you learn some names and that you know what the ingredients are so that you will not offend your host by not eating what they are serving. Remember that cooking is an expression of love and patience for Arab culture.

5. Listen carefully and learn more about local rules and norms regarding family traditions, adoption of children, poverty level, wedding celebrations, use of a driver, breaking the silence of abusive domestic situations among other socio-cultural ambiguities of the Kingdom.

6. Absorb the facts of the high-value women place on beauty and fashion. Do not question the use of make-up. The use of make-up is synonymous with being a progressive woman in society. It is freedom representation.

7. Be aware of the moral police. Islamic religious police is an official government body that enforces religious observance and public morality on behalf of national or regional authorities based on its interpretation of Sharia.

8. Follow the dress code of the country without question. Remember, Saudi women were born under a specific dress pattern and regulations, and they have embraced it as a standard way of living. You must abide by the dress code rules without hesitation.

9. Gain knowledge of the prohibitions on alcohol consumption. Do not fall into the temptation of making it, purchasing it from others who are smuggling it or risking your life by bringing it inside the country.

10. Respect the prayer time. Foreigners must preserve the spiritual atmosphere in the country. If you profess a different religion from Islam, inform yourself on how you can legally join others who attend the religion services of your faith.

11. Go with the flow. There will always be minor or significant inconveniences that you will experience in the Kingdom. Take a deep breath, let it go and enjoy the experience.

12. Avoid overpacking! You can find everything in the Kingdom. They import a variety of products from markets worldwide. Bring the essential items that are generally difficult to locate (i.e., specific hair and skin products).

13. Familiarize yourself with simple Arabic everyday words and phrases. Making an effort to learn the language is meaningful and appreciated.

For *Spiritual Reasons*:

1. Know that only Muslims can visit Mecca and Medina.

2. Practicing your religion can be complicated unless you have information on where and when people who profess your faith gather for praying.

3. Learn about the social interpretation of the Quran and the use of the Holy book as the government constitution ruling the country.

4. Realize that women have specific roles in Islam. If you visit a Mosque, do not express surprise on the location inside the Mosque where women practice their Muslim faith.

5. Respect the language of spirituality voiced by all people professing Islam.

6. Understand the degree of commitment of religious practices imposed on all individuals on Fridays, Mosque day.

7. Plan your internal house chores on Fridays around the time that businesses close for prayer time.

8. Learn and understand the meaning of Ramadan, the importance of fasting as one of the Five Pillars of Islam. Adapt your regular schedule of personal activities around the fasting time during the daylight hours from dawn to sunset.

9. Do not eat or drink in public during Ramadan.

10. Be aware that hugging and kissing are in no way acceptable during Ramadan while fasting. However, you may find different interpretations that would indicate that it is permissible if it does not sexually "move" a person.

11. Refrain from talking about religion or politics in any place in the Kingdom of Saudi Arabia.

Made in the USA
Lexington, KY
05 December 2019